1991

Levitt on Marketing

LEVITT ON MARKETING

A Harvard Business Review Paperback

Harvard Business Review paperback No. 90056
ISBN 0-87584-284-4

The *Harvard Business Review* articles in this collection
are available individually. Discounts apply to quantity
purchases. For information and ordering contact Operations Department, Harvard Business School Publishing
Division, Boston, MA 02163. Telephone: (617) 495-6192,
9 a.m. to 5 p.m. Eastern Standard Time, Monday through
Friday. Fax: (617) 495-6985, 24 hours a day.

Editor's Note: Some articles in this book may have been written before authors and editors began to take into consideration the role of women in management. We hope the archaic
usage representing all managers as male does not detract from
the usefulness of the collection.

Printed in the United States of America by Harvard University, Office of the University Publisher.
93 92 91   5 4 3 2 1

Contents

Product Differentiation

If marketing managers apply sufficient imagination and alertness, they can differentiate even price-sensitive commodities.

Many products and most services have intangible benefits. Identifying and using them will help companies get customers and hold them.

Service Marketing

The rigid distinction between products and services serves no purpose. Everybody is in services. And customer-service activities and service organizations will benefit from judicious application of manufacturing methods and thinking.

Quality can be improved by using machinery or organized systems to overhaul labor-intensive services—but many untapped opportunities remain.

The Marketing Concept

HBR Classic

Shortsighted managements often fail to recognize that in fact there is no such thing as a growth industry

How can a company ensure its continued growth? In 1960 "Marketing Myopia" answered that question in a new and challenging way by urging organizations to define their industries broadly to take advantage of growth opportunities. Using the archetype of the railroads, Mr. Levitt showed how they declined inevitably as technology advanced because they defined themselves too narrowly. To continue growing, companies must ascertain and act on their customers' needs and desires, not bank on the presumptive longevity of their products. The success of the article testifies to the validity of its message. It has been widely quoted and anthologized, and HBR has sold more than 265,000 reprints of it. The author of 14 subsequent articles in HBR, Mr. Levitt is one of the magazine's most prolific contributors. In a retrospective commentary, he considers the use and misuse that have been made of "Marketing Myopia," describing its many interpretations and hypothesizing about its success.

At the time of the article's publication, Theodore Levitt was lecturer in business administration at the Harvard Business School. Now a full professor there, he is the author of six books, including The Third Sector: New Tactics for a Responsive Society *(1973) and* Marketing for Business Growth *(1974).*

Theodore Levitt

Marketing myopia

Every major industry was once a growth industry. But some that are now riding a wave of growth enthusiasm are very much in the shadow of decline. Others which are thought of as seasoned growth industries have actually stopped growing. In every case the reason growth is threatened, slowed, or stopped is *not* because the market is saturated. It is because there has been a failure of management.

Fateful purposes: The failure is at the top. The executives responsible for it, in the last analysis, are those who deal with broad aims and policies. Thus:

□
The railroads did not stop growing because the need for passenger and freight transportation declined. That grew. The railroads are in trouble today not because the need was filled by others (cars, trucks, airplanes, even telephones), but because it was *not* filled by the railroads themselves. They let others take customers away from them because they assumed themselves to be in the railroad business rather than in the transportation business. The reason they defined their industry wrong was because they were railroad-oriented instead of transportation-oriented; they were product-oriented instead of customer-oriented.

□
Hollywood barely escaped being totally ravished by television. Actually, all the established film companies went through drastic reorganizations. Some simply disappeared. All of them got into trouble not because of TV's inroads but because of their own myopia. As with the railroads, Hollywood defined its business incorrectly. It thought it was in the movie business when it was actually in the entertainment business. "Movies" implied a specific, limited product. This produced a fatuous contentment which from the beginning led producers to view TV as a threat. Hollywood scorned and rejected TV when it should have welcomed it as an opportunity—an opportunity to expand the entertainment business.

Today TV is a bigger business than the old narrowly defined movie business ever was. Had Hollywood been customer-oriented (providing entertainment), rather then product-oriented (making movies), would it have gone through the fiscal purgatory that it did? I doubt it. What ultimately saved Hollywood and accounted for its recent resurgence was the wave of new young writers, producers, and directors whose previous successes in television had decimated the old movie companies and toppled the big movie moguls.

There are other less obvious examples of industries that have been and are now endangering their futures by improperly defining their purposes. I shall discuss some in detail later and analyze the kind of policies that lead to trouble. Right now it may help to show what a thoroughly customer-oriented management *can* do to keep a growth industry growing, even after the obvious opportunities have been exhausted; and here there are two examples that have been around for a long time. They are nylon and glass—specifically, E. I. duPont de Nemours & Company and Corning Glass Works.

Both companies have great technical competence. Their product orientation is unquestioned. But this alone does not explain their success. After all, who was more pridefully product-oriented and product-conscious than the erstwhile New England textile companies that have been so thoroughly massacred? The DuPonts and the Cornings have succeeded not primarily because of their product or research orientation but because they have been thoroughly customer-oriented also. It is constant watchfulness for opportunities to apply their technical know-how to the creation of customer-satisfying uses which accounts for their prodigious output of successful new products. Without a very sophisticated eye on the customer, most of their new products might have been wrong, their sales methods useless.

Aluminum has also continued to be a growth industry, thanks to the efforts of two wartime-created companies which deliberately set about creating new customer-satisfying uses. Without Kaiser Aluminum & Chemical Corporation and Reynolds Metals

Company, the total demand for aluminum today would be vastly less.

Error of analysis: Some may argue that it is foolish to set the railroads off against aluminum or the movies off against glass. Are not aluminum and glass naturally so versatile that the industries are bound to have more growth opportunities than the railroads and movies? This view commits precisely the error I have been talking about. It defines an industry, or a product, or a cluster of know-how so narrowly as to guarantee its premature senescence. When we mention "railroads," we should make sure we mean "transportation." As transporters, the railroads still have a good chance for very considerable growth. They are not limited to the railroad business as such (though in my opinion rail transportation is potentially a much stronger transportation medium than is generally believed).

What the railroads lack is not opportunity, but some of the same managerial imaginativeness and audacity that made them great. Even an amateur like Jacques Barzun can see what is lacking when he says:

"I grieve to see the most advanced physical and social organization of the last century go down in shabby disgrace for lack of the same comprehensive imagination that built it up. [What is lacking is] the will of the companies to survive and to satisfy the public by inventiveness and skill." [1]

Shadow of obsolescence

It is impossible to mention a single major industry that did not at one time qualify for the magic appellation of "growth industry." In each case its assumed strength lay in the apparently unchallenged superiority of its product. There appeared to be no effective substitute for it. It was itself a runaway substitute for the product it so triumphantly replaced. Yet one after another of these celebrated industries has come under a shadow. Let us look briefly at a few more of them, this time taking examples that have so far received a little less attention:

☐
Dry cleaning—This was once a growth industry with lavish prospects. In an age of wool garments, imagine being finally able to get them safely and easily clean. The boom was on.

Yet here we are 30 years after the boom started and the industry is in trouble. Where has the competition come from? From a better way of cleaning? No. It has come from synthetic fibers and chemical additives that have cut the need for dry cleaning. But this is only the beginning. Lurking in the wings and ready to make chemical dry cleaning totally obsolescent is that powerful magician, ultrasonics.

☐
Electric utilities— This is another one of those supposedly "no-substitute" products that has been enthroned on a pedestal of invincible growth. When the incandescent lamp came along, kerosene lights were finished. Later the water wheel and the steam engine were cut to ribbons by the flexibility, reliability, simplicity, and just plain easy availability of electric motors. The prosperity of electric utilities continues to wax extravagant as the home is converted into a museum of electric gadgetry. How can anybody miss by investing in utilities, with no competition, nothing but growth ahead?

But a second look is not quite so comforting. A score of nonutility companies are well advanced toward developing a powerful chemical fuel cell which could sit in some hidden closet of every home silently ticking off electric power. The electric lines that vulgarize so many neighborhoods will be eliminated. So will the endless demolition of streets and service interruptions during storms. Also on the horizon is solar energy, again pioneered by nonutility companies.

Who says that the utilities have no competition? They may be natural monopolies now, but tomorrow they may be natural deaths. To avoid this prospect, they too will have to develop fuel cells, solar energy, and other power sources. To survive, they themselves will have to plot the obsolescence of what now produces their livelihood.

□

Grocery stores—Many people find it hard to realize that there ever was a thriving establishment known as the "corner grocery store." The supermarket has taken over with a powerful effectiveness. Yet the big food chains of the 1930s narrowly escaped being completely wiped out by the aggressive expansion of independent supermarkets. The first genuine supermarket was opened in 1930, in Jamaica, Long Island. By 1933 supermarkets were thriving in California, Ohio, Pennsylvania, and elsewhere. Yet the established chains pompously ignored them. When they chose to notice them, it was with such derisive descriptions as "cheapy," "horse-and-buggy," "cracker-barrel storekeeping," and "unethical opportunists."

The executive of one big chain announced at the time that he found it "hard to believe that people will drive for miles to shop for foods and sacrifice the personal service chains have perfected and to which Mrs. Consumer is accustomed." [2] As late as 1936, the National Wholesale Grocers convention and the New Jersey Retail Grocers Association said there was nothing to fear. They said that the supers' narrow appeal to the price buyer limited the size of their market. They had to draw from miles around. When imitators came, there would be wholesale liquidations as volume fell. The current high sales of the supers was said to be partly due to their novelty. Basically people wanted convenient neighborhood grocers. If the neighborhood stores "cooperate with their suppliers, pay attention to their costs, and improve their service," they would be able to weather the competition until it blew over.[3]

It never blew over. The chains discovered that survival required going into the supermarket business. This meant the wholesale destruction of their huge investments in corner store sites and in established distribution and merchandising methods. The companies with "the courage of their convictions" resolutely stuck to the corner store philosophy. They kept their pride but lost their shirts.

Self-deceiving cycle: But memories are short. For example, it is hard for people who today confidently hail the twin messiahs of electronics and chemicals to see how things could possibly go wrong with these galloping industries. They probably also cannot see how a reasonably sensible businessman could have been as myopic as the famous Boston millionaire who 50 years ago unintentionally sentenced his heirs to poverty by stipulating that his entire estate be forever invested exclusively in electric streetcar securities. His posthumous declaration, "There will always be a big demand for efficient urban transportation," is no consolation to his heirs who sustain life by pumping gasoline at automobile filling stations.

Yet, in a casual survey I recently took among a group of intelligent business executives, nearly half agreed that it would be hard to hurt their heirs by tying their estates forever to the electronics industry. When I then confronted them with the Boston streetcar example, they chorused unanimously, "That's different!" But is it? Is not the basic situation identical?

In truth, *there is no such thing* as a growth industry, I believe. There are only companies organized and operated to create and capitalize on growth opportunities. Industries that assume themselves to be riding some automatic growth escalator invariably descend into stagnation. The history of every dead and dying "growth" industry shows a self-deceiving cycle of bountiful expansion and undetected decay. There are four conditions which usually guarantee this cycle:

1
The belief that growth is assured by an expanding and more affluent population.

2
The belief that there is no competitive substitute for the industry's major product.

3
Too much faith in mass production and in the advantages of rapidly declining unit costs as output rises.

4
Preoccupation with a product that lends itself to carefully controlled scientific experimentation, improvement, and manufacturing cost reduction.

I should like now to begin examining each of these conditions in some detail. To build my case as boldly as possible, I shall illustrate the points with reference to three industries—petroleum, automobiles, and electronics—particularly petroleum, because it spans more years and more vicissitudes. Not only do these three have excellent reputations with the general public and also enjoy the confidence of sophisticated investors, but their managements have become known for progressive thinking in areas like financial control, product research, and management training. If obsolescence can cripple even these industries, it can happen anywhere.

Population myth

The belief that profits are assured by an expanding and more affluent population is dear to the heart of every industry. It takes the edge off the apprehensions everybody understandably feels about the future. If consumers are multiplying and also buying more of your product or service, you can face the future with considerably more comfort than if the market is shrinking. An expanding market keeps the manufacturer from having to think very hard or imaginatively. If thinking is an intellectual response to a problem, then the absence of a problem leads to the absence of thinking. If your product has an automatically expanding market, then you will not give much thought to how to expand it.

One of the most interesting examples of this is provided by the petroleum

1. Jacques Barzun, "Trains and the Mind of Man," *Holiday*, February 1960, p. 21.

2. For more details see M. M. Zimmerman, *The Super Market: A Revolution in Distribution* (New York, McGraw-Hill Book Company, Inc., 1955), p. 48.

3. Ibid., pp. 45–47.

industry. Probably our oldest growth industry, it has an enviable record. While there are some current apprehensions about its growth rate, the industry itself tends to be optimistic.

But I believe it can be demonstrated that it is undergoing a fundamental yet typical change. It is not only ceasing to be a growth industry, but may actually be a declining one, relative to other business. Although there is widespread unawareness of it, I believe that within 25 years the oil industry may find itself in much the same position of retrospective glory that the railroads are now in. Despite its pioneering work in developing and applying the present-value method of investment evaluation, in employee relations, and in working with backward countries, the petroleum business is a distressing example of how complacency and wrongheadedness can stubbornly convert opportunity into near disaster.

One of the characteristics of this and other industries that have believed very strongly in the beneficial consequences of an expanding population, while at the same time being industries with a generic product for which there has appeared to be no competitive substitute, is that the individual companies have sought to outdo their competitors by improving on what they are already doing. This makes sense, of course, if one assumes that sales are tied to the country's population strings, because the customer can compare products only on a feature-by-feature basis. I believe it is significant, for example, that not since John D. Rockefeller sent free kerosene lamps to China has the oil industry done anything really outstanding to create a demand for its product. Not even in product improvement has it showered itself with eminence. The greatest single improvement—namely, the development of tetraethyl lead—came from outside the industry, specifically from General Motors and DuPont. The big contributions made by the industry itself are confined to the technology of oil exploration, production, and refining.

4. *The Affluent Society* (Boston, Houghton Mifflin Company, 1958), pp. 152-160.

Asking for trouble: In other words, the industry's efforts have focused on improving the *efficiency* of getting and making its product, not really on improving the generic product or its marketing. Moreover, its chief product has continuously been defined in the narrowest possible terms, namely, gasoline, not energy, fuel, or transportation. This attitude has helped assure that:

○

Major improvements in gasoline quality tend not to originate in the oil industry. Also, the development of superior alternative fuels comes from outside the oil industry, as will be shown later.

○

Major innovations in automobile fuel marketing are originated by small new oil companies that are not primarily preoccupied with production or refining. These are the companies that have been responsible for the rapidly expanding multipump gasoline stations, with their successful emphasis on large and clean layouts, rapid and efficient driveway service, and quality gasoline at low prices.

Thus, the oil industry is asking for trouble from outsiders. Sooner or later, in this land of hungry inventors and entrepreneurs, a threat is sure to come. The possibilities of this will become more apparent when we turn to the next dangerous belief of many managements. For the sake of continuity, because this second belief is tied closely to the first, I shall continue with the same example.

Idea of indispensability: The petroleum industry is pretty much persuaded that there is no competitive substitute for its major product, gasoline—or if there is, that it will continue to be a derivative of crude oil, such as diesel fuel or kerosene jet fuel.

There is a lot of automatic wishful thinking in this assumption. The trouble is that most refining companies own huge amounts of crude oil reserves. These have value only if there is a market for products into which oil can be converted—hence the tenacious belief in the continuing competitive superiority of automobile fuels made from crude oil.

This idea persists despite all historic evidence against it. The evidence not only shows that oil has never been a superior product for any purpose for very long, but it also shows that the oil industry has never really been a growth industry. It has been a succession of different businesses that have gone through the usual historic cycles of growth, maturity, and decay. Its overall survival is owed to a series of miraculous escapes from total obsolescence, of last-minute and unexpected reprieves from total disaster reminiscent of the Perils of Pauline.

Perils of petroleum: I shall sketch in only the main episodes.

First, crude oil was largely a patent medicine. But even before that fad ran out, demand was greatly expanded by the use of oil in kerosene lamps. The prospect of lighting the world's lamps gave rise to an extravagant promise of growth. The prospects were similar to those the industry now holds for gasoline in other parts of the world. It can hardly wait for the underdeveloped nations to get a car in every garage.

In the days of the kerosene lamp, the oil companies competed with each other and against gaslight by trying to improve the illuminating characteristics of kerosene. Then suddenly the impossible happened. Edison invented a light which was totally nondependent on crude oil. Had it not been for the growing use of kerosene in space heaters, the incandescent lamp would have completely finished oil as a growth industry at that time. Oil would have been good for little else than axle grease.

Then disaster and reprieve struck again. Two great innovations occurred, neither originating in the oil industry. The successful development of coal-burning domestic central-heating systems made the space heater obsolescent. While the industry reeled, along came its most magnificent boost yet—the internal combustion engine, also invented by outsiders. Then when the prodigious expansion for gasoline finally began to level off in the 1920s, along came the miraculous escape of a central oil heater. Once again, the escape was provided by an outsider's invention and development. And when that market weakened, wartime demand for aviation fuel came to the rescue. After the war the expansion of civilian aviation, the dieselization of railroads, and the explosive demand for cars and trucks kept the industry's growth in high gear.

Meanwhile, centralized oil heating—whose boom potential had only recently been proclaimed—ran into severe competition from natural gas. While the oil companies themselves owned the gas that now competed with their oil, the industry did not originate the natural gas revolution, nor has it to this day greatly profited from its gas ownership. The gas revolution was made by newly formed transmission companies that marketed the product with an aggressive ardor. They started a magnificent new industry, first against the advice and then against the resistance of the oil companies.

By all the logic of the situation, the oil companies themselves should have made the gas revolution. They not only owned the gas; they also were the only people experienced in handling, scrubbing, and using it, the only people experienced in pipeline technology and transmission, and they understood heating problems. But, partly because they knew that natural gas would compete with their own sale of heating oil, the oil companies pooh-poohed the potentials of gas.

The revolution was finally started by oil pipeline executives who, unable to persuade their own companies to go into gas, quit and organized the spectacularly successful gas transmission companies. Even after their success became painfully evident to the oil companies, the latter did not go into gas transmission. The multibillion dollar business which should have been theirs went to others. As in the past, the industry was blinded by its narrow preoccupation with a specific product and the value of its reserves. It paid little or no attention to its customers' basic needs and preferences.

The postwar years have not witnessed any change. Immediately after World War II the oil industry was greatly encouraged about its future by the rapid expansion of demand for its traditional line of products. In 1950 most companies projected annual rates of domestic expansion of around 6% through at least 1975. Though the ratio of crude oil reserves to demand in the Free World was about 20 to 1, with 10 to 1 being usually considered a reasonable working ratio in the United States, booming demand sent oil men searching for more without sufficient regard to what the future really promised. In 1952 they "hit" in the Middle East; the ratio skyrocketed to 42 to 1. If gross additions to reserves continue at the average rate of the past five years (37 billion barrels annually), then by 1970 the reserve ratio will be up to 45 to 1. This abundance of oil has weakened crude and product prices all over the world.

Uncertain future: Management cannot find much consolation today in the rapidly expanding petrochemical industry, another oil-using idea that did not originate in the leading firms. The total United States production of petrochemicals is equivalent to about 2% (by volume) of the demand for all petroleum products. Although the petrochemical industry is now expected to grow by about 10% per year, this will not offset other drains on the growth of crude oil consumption. Furthermore, while petrochemical products are many and growing, it is well to remember that there are nonpetroleum sources of the basic raw material, such as coal. Besides, a lot of plastics can be produced with relatively little oil. A 50,000-barrel-per-day oil refinery is now considered the absolute minimum size for efficiency. But a 5,000-barrel-per-day chemical plant is a giant operation.

Oil has never been a continuously strong growth industry. It has grown by fits and starts, always miraculously saved by innovations and developments not of its own making. The reason it has not grown in a smooth progression is that each time it thought it had a superior product safe from the possibility of competitive substitutes, the product turned out to be inferior and notoriously subject to obsolescence. Until now, gasoline (for motor fuel, anyhow) has escaped this fate. But, as we shall see later, it too may be on its last legs.

The point of all this is that there is no guarantee against product obsolescence. If a company's own research does not make it obsolete, another's will. Unless an industry is especially lucky, as oil has been until now, it can easily go down in a sea of red figures—just as the railroads have, as the buggy whip manufacturers have, as the corner grocery chains have, as most of the big movie companies have, and indeed as many other industries have.

The best way for a firm to be lucky is to make its own luck. That requires knowing what makes a business successful. One of the greatest enemies of this knowledge is mass production.

Production pressures

Mass-production industries are impelled by a great drive to produce all they can. The prospect of steeply declining unit costs as output rises is more than most companies can usually resist. The profit possibilities look spectacular. All effort focuses on production. The result is that marketing gets neglected.

John Kenneth Galbraith contends that just the opposite occurs.[4] Output is so prodigious that all effort concentrates on trying to get rid of it. He says this accounts for singing commercials, desecration of the countryside with advertising signs, and other wasteful and vulgar practices. Galbraith has a finger on something real, but he misses the strategic point. Mass production does indeed generate great pressure to "move" the product. But what usually gets emphasized is selling, not marketing. Marketing, being a more sophisticated and complex process, gets ignored.

The difference between marketing and selling is more than semantic. Selling focuses on the needs of the seller, marketing on the needs of the buyer. Selling is preoccupied with the seller's need to convert his product into cash, marketing with the idea of satisfying the needs of the customer by means of the product and the whole cluster of things associated with creating, delivering, and finally consuming it.

In some industries the enticements of full mass production have been so powerful that for many years top management in effect has told the sales departments, "You get rid of it; we'll worry about profits." By contrast, a truly marketing-minded firm tries to create value-satisfying goods and services that consumers will want to buy. What it offers for sale includes not only the generic product or service, but also how it is made available to the customer, in what form, when, under what conditions, and at what terms of trade. Most important, what it offers for sale is determined not by the seller but by the buyer. The seller takes his cues from the buyer in such a way that the product becomes a consequence of the marketing effort, not vice versa.

Lag in Detroit: This may sound like an elementary rule of business, but that does not keep it from being violated wholesale. It is certainly more violated than honored. Take the automobile industry.

Here mass production is most famous, most honored, and has the greatest impact on the entire society. The industry has hitched its fortune to the relentless requirements of the annual model change, a policy that makes customer orientation an especially urgent necessity. Consequently the auto companies annually spend millions of dollars on consumer research. But the fact that the new compact cars are selling so well in their first year indicates that Detroit's vast researches have for a long time failed to reveal what the customer really wanted. Detroit was not persuaded that he wanted anything different from what he had been getting until it lost millions of

customers to other small car manufacturers.

How could this unbelievable lag behind consumer wants have been perpetuated so long? Why did not research reveal consumer preferences before consumers' buying decisions themselves revealed the facts? Is that not what consumer research is for—to find out before the fact what is going to happen? The answer is that Detroit never really researched the customer's wants. It only researched his preferences between the kinds of things which it had already decided to offer him. For Detroit is mainly product-oriented, not customer-oriented. To the extent that the customer is recognized as having needs that the manufacturer should try to satisfy, Detroit usually acts as if the job can be done entirely by product changes. Occasionally attention gets paid to financing, too, but that is done more in order to sell than to enable the customer to buy.

As for taking care of other customer needs, there is not enough being done to write about. The areas of the greatest unsatisfied needs are ignored, or at best get stepchild attention. These are at the point of sale and on the matter of automative repair and maintenance. Detroit views these problem areas as being of secondary importance. That is underscored by the fact that the retailing and servicing ends of this industry are neither owned and operated nor controlled by the manufacturers. Once the car is produced, things are pretty much in the dealer's inadequate hands. Illustrative of Detroit's arm's-length attitude is the fact that, while servicing holds enormous sales-stimulating, profit-building opportunities, only 57 of Chevrolet's 7,000 dealers provide night maintenance service.

Motorists repeatedly express their dissatisfaction with servicing and their apprehensions about buying cars under the present selling setup. The anxieties and problems they encounter during the auto buying and maintenance processes are probably more intense and widespread today than 30 years ago. Yet the automobile companies do not *seem* to listen to or take their cues

from the anguished consumer. If they do listen, it must be through the filter of their own preoccupation with production. The marketing effort is still viewed as a necessary consequence of the product, not vice versa, as it should be. That is the legacy of mass production, with its parochial view that profit resides essentially in low-cost full production.

What Ford put first: The profit lure of mass production obviously has a place in the plans and strategy of business management, but it must always *follow* hard thinking about the customer. This is one of the most important lessons that we can learn from the contradictory behavior of Henry Ford. In a sense Ford was both the most brilliant and the most senseless marketer in American history. He was senseless because he refused to give the customer anything but a black car. He was brilliant because he fashioned a production system designed to fit market needs. We habitually celebrate him for the wrong reason, his production genius. His real genius was marketing. We think he was able to cut his selling price and therefore sell millions of $500 cars because his invention of the assembly line had reduced the costs. Actually he invented the assembly line because he had concluded that at $500 he could sell millions of cars. Mass production was the *result* not the cause of his low prices.

Ford repeatedly emphasized this point, but a nation of production-oriented business managers refuses to hear the great lesson he taught. Here is his operating philosophy as he expressed it succinctly:

"Our policy is to reduce the price, extend the operations, and improve the article. You will notice that the reduction of price comes first. We have never considered any costs as fixed. Therefore we first reduce the price to the point where we believe more sales will result. Then we go ahead and try to make the prices. We do not bother about the costs. The new price forces the costs down. The more usual way is to take the costs and then determine the price; and although that method may be scientific in the narrow sense, it is not scientific in the broad sense, because what earthly use is it to know the·cost if it tells you that you cannot manufacture at a price at which the article can be sold? But more to the point is the fact that, although one may calculate what a cost is, and of course all of our costs are carefully calculated, no one knows what a cost ought to be. One of the ways of discovering... is to name a price so low as to force everybody in the place to the highest point of efficiency. The low price makes everybody dig for profits. We make more discoveries concerning manufacturing and selling under this forced method than by any method of leisurely investigation." [5]

Product provincialism: The tantalizing profit possibilities of low unit production costs may be the most seriously self-deceiving attitude that can afflict a company, particularly a "growth" company where an apparently assured expansion of demand already tends to undermine a proper concern for the importance of marketing and the customer.

The usual result of this narrow preoccupation with so-called concrete matters is that instead of growing, the industry declines. It usually means that the product fails to adapt to the constantly changing patterns of consumer needs and tastes, to new and modified marketing institutions and practices, or to product developments in competing or complementary industries. The industry has its eyes so firmly on its own specific product that it does not see how it is being made obsolete.

The classical example of this is the buggy whip industry. No amount of product improvement could stave off its death sentence. But had the industry defined itself as being in the transportation business rather than the buggy whip business, it might have survived. It would have done what survival always entails, that is, changing. Even if it had only defined its business as providing a stimulant or catalyst to an energy source, it might

5. Henry Ford, *My Life and Work* (New York, Doubleday, Page & Company, 1923), pp. 146-147.

have survived by becoming a manufacturer of, say, fanbelts or air cleaners.

What may some day be a still more classical example is, again, the oil industry. Having let others steal marvelous opportunities from it (e.g., natural gas, as already mentioned, missile fuels, and jet engine lubricants), one would expect it to have taken steps never to let that happen again. But this is not the case. We are now getting extraordinary new developments in fuel systems specifically designed to power automobiles. Not only are these developments concentrated in firms outside the petroleum industry, but petroleum is almost systematically ignoring them, securely content in its wedded bliss to oil. It is the story of the kerosene lamp versus the incandescent lamp all over again. Oil is trying to improve hydrocarbon fuels rather than develop *any* fuels best suited to the needs of their users, whether or not made in different ways and with different raw materials from oil.

Here are some things which nonpetroleum companies are working on:

☐

Over a dozen such firms now have advanced working models of energy systems which, when perfected, will replace the internal combustion engine and eliminate the demand for gasoline. The superior merit of each of these systems is their elimination of frequent, time-consuming, and irritating refueling stops. Most of these systems are fuel cells designed to create electrical energy directly from chemicals without combustion. Most of them use chemicals that are not derived from oil, generally hydrogen and oxygen.

☐

Several other companies have advanced models of electric storage batteries designed to power automobiles. One of these is an aircraft producer that is working jointly with several electric utility companies. The latter hope to use off-peak generating capacity to supply overnight plug-in battery regeneration. Another company, also using the battery approach, is a medium-size electronics firm with extensive small-battery experience that it

developed in connection with its work on hearing aids. It is collaborating with an automobile manufacturer. Recent improvements arising from the need for high-powered miniature power storage plants in rockets have put us within reach of a relatively small battery capable of withstanding great overloads or surges of power. Germanium diode applications and batteries using sintered-plate and nickel-cadmium techniques promise to make a revolution in our energy sources.

☐

Solar energy conversion systems are also getting increasing attention. One usually cautious Detroit auto executive recently ventured that solar-powered cars might be common by 1980.

As for the oil companies, they are more or less "watching developments," as one research director put it to me. A few are doing a bit of research on fuel cells, but almost always confined to developing cells powered by hydrocarbon chemicals. None of them are enthusiastically researching fuel cells, batteries, or solar power plants. None of them are spending a fraction as much on research in these profoundly important areas as they are on the usual run-of-the-mill things like reducing combustion chamber deposit in gasoline engines. One major integrated petroleum company recently took a tentative look at the fuel cell and concluded that although "the companies actively working on it indicate a belief in ultimate success... the timing and magnitude of its impact are too remote to warrant recognition in our forecasts."

One might, of course, ask: Why should the oil companies do anything different? Would not chemical fuel cells, batteries, or solar energy kill the present product lines? The answer is that they would indeed, and that is precisely the reason for the oil firms having to develop these power units before their competitors, so they will not be companies without an industry.

Management might be more likely to do what is needed for its own preservation if it thought of itself as being in the energy business. But even that would not be enough if it persists in imprisoning itself in the narrow grip of its tight product orientation. It has to think of itself as taking care of customer needs, not finding, refining, or even selling oil. Once it genuinely thinks of its business as taking care of people's transportation needs, nothing can stop it from creating its own extravagantly profitable growth.

'Creative destruction': Since words are cheap and deeds are dear, it may be appropriate to indicate what this kind of thinking involves and leads to. Let us start at the beginning—the customer. It can be shown that motorists strongly dislike the bother, delay, and experience of buying gasoline. People actually do not buy gasoline. They cannot see it, taste it, feel it, appreciate it, or really test it. What they buy is the right to continue driving their cars. The gas station is like a tax collector to whom people are compelled to pay a periodic toll as the price of using their cars. This makes the gas station a basically unpopular institution. It can never be made popular or pleasant, only less unpopular, less unpleasant.

To reduce its unpopularity completely means eliminating it. Nobody likes a tax collector, not even a pleasantly cheerful one. Nobody likes to interrupt a trip to buy a phantom product, not even from a handsome Adonis or a seductive Venus. Hence, companies that are working on exotic fuel substitutes which will eliminate the need for frequent refueling are heading directly into the outstretched arms of the irritated motorist. They are riding a wave of inevitability, not because they are creating something which is technologically superior or more sophisticated, but because they are satisfying a powerful customer need. They are also eliminating noxious odors and air pollution.

Once the petroleum companies recognize the customer-satisfying logic of what another power system can do, they will see that they have no more choice about working on an efficient, long-lasting fuel (or some way of delivering present fuels without bothering the motorist) than the big food

chains had a choice about going into the supermarket business, or the vacuum tube companies had a choice about making semiconductors. For their own good the oil firms will have to destroy their own highly profitable assets. No amount of wishful thinking can save them from the necessity of engaging in this form of "creative destruction."

I phrase the need as strongly as this because I think management must make quite an effort to break itself loose from conventional ways. It is all too easy in this day and age for a company or industry to let its sense of purpose become dominated by the economies of full production and to develop a dangerously lopsided product orientation. In short, if management lets itself drift, it invariably drifts in the direction of thinking of itself as producing goods and services, not customer satisfactions. While it probably will not descend to the depths of telling its salesmen, "You get rid of it; we'll worry about profits," it can, without knowing it, be practicing precisely that formula for withering decay. The historic fate of one growth industry after another has been its suicidal product provincialism.

Dangers of R&D

Another big danger to a firm's continued growth arises when top management is wholly transfixed by the profit possibilities of technical research and development. To illustrate I shall turn first to a new industry—electronics—and then return once more to the oil companies. By comparing a fresh example with a familiar one, I hope to emphasize the prevalence and insidiousness of a hazardous way of thinking.

Marketing shortchanged: In the case of electronics, the greatest danger which faces the glamorous new companies in this field is not that they do not pay enough attention to research and development, but that they pay *too much* attention to it. And the fact that the fastest growing electronics firms owe their eminence to their heavy emphasis on technical research

is completely beside the point. They have vaulted to affluence on a sudden crest of unusually strong general receptiveness to new technical ideas. Also, their success has been shaped in the virtually guaranteed market of military subsidies and by military orders that in many cases actually preceded the existence of facilities to make the products. Their expansion has, in other words, been almost totally devoid of marketing effort.

Thus, they are growing up under conditions that come dangerously close to creating the illusion that a superior product will sell itself. Having created a successful company by making a superior product, it is not surprising that management continues to be oriented toward the product rather than the people who consume it. It develops the philosophy that continued growth is a matter of continued product innovation and improvement.

A number of other factors tend to strengthen and sustain this belief:

1

Because electronic products are highly complex and sophisticated, managements become top-heavy with engineers and scientists. This creates a selective bias in favor of research and production at the expense of marketing. The organization tends to view itself as making things rather than satisfying customer needs. Marketing gets treated as a residual activity, "something else" that must be done once the vital job of product creation and production is completed.

2

To this bias in favor of product research, development, and production is added the bias in favor of dealing with controllable variables. Engineers and scientists are at home in the world of concrete things like machines, test tubes, production lines, and even balance sheets. The abstractions to which they feel kindly are those which are testable or manipulatable in the laboratory, or, if not testable, then functional, such as Euclid's axioms. In short, the managements of the new glamour-growth companies tend to favor those business activities which lend themselves to careful study, experimentation, and control—the hard, practical realities of the lab, the shop, the books.

What gets shortchanged are the realities of the *market*. Consumers are unpredictable, varied, fickle, stupid, shortsighted, stubborn, and generally bothersome. This is not what the engineer-managers say, but deep down in their consciousness it is what they believe. And this accounts for their concentrating on what they know and what they can control, namely, product research, engineering, and production. The emphasis on production becomes particularly attractive when the product can be made at declining unit costs. There is no more inviting way of making money than by running the plant full blast.

Today the top-heavy science-engineering-production orientation of so many electronics companies works reasonably well because they are pushing into new frontiers in which the armed services have pioneered virtually assured markets. The companies are in the felicitous position of having to fill, not find markets; of not having to discover what the customer needs and wants, but of having the customer voluntarily come forward with specific new product demands. If a team of consultants had been assigned specifically to design a business situation calculated to prevent the emergence and development of a customer-oriented marketing viewpoint, it could not have produced anything better than the conditions just described.

Stepchild treatment: The oil industry is a stunning example of how science, technology, and mass production can divert an entire group of companies from their main task. To the extent the consumer is studied at all (which is not much), the focus is forever on getting information which is designed to help the oil companies improve what they are now doing. They try to discover more convincing advertising themes, more effective sales promotional drives, what the market shares of the various companies are, what people like or dislike about service station dealers and oil companies, and so forth. Nobody seems as interested in probing deeply into the basic human needs that the industry might be trying to satisfy as in probing into the basic properties of the raw material that the companies work with in trying to deliver customer satisfactions.

Basic questions about customers and markets seldom get asked. The latter occupy a stepchild status. They are recognized as existing, as having to be taken care of, but not worth very much real thought or dedicated attention. Nobody gets as excited about the customers in his own backyard as about the oil in the Sahara Desert. Nothing illustrates better the neglect of marketing than its treatment in the industry press.

The centennial issue of the *American Petroleum Institute Quarterly*, published in 1959 to celebrate the discovery of oil in Titusville, Pennsylvania, contained 21 feature articles proclaiming the industry's greatness. Only one of these talked about its achievements in marketing, and that was only a pictorial record of how service station architecture has changed. The issue also contained a special section on "New Horizons," which was devoted to showing the magnificent role oil would play in America's future. Every reference was ebulliently optimistic, never implying once that oil might have some hard competition. Even the reference to atomic energy was a cheerful catalogue of how oil would help make atomic energy a success. There was not a single apprehension that the oil industry's affluence might be threatened or a suggestion that one "new horizon" might include new and better ways of serving oil's present customers.

But the most revealing example of the stepchild treatment that marketing gets was still another special series of short articles on "The Revolutionary Potential of Electronics." Under that heading this list of articles appeared in the table of contents:

○
"In the Search for Oil"
○
"In Production Operations"
○
"In Refinery Processes"
○
"In Pipeline Operations"

Significantly, every one of the industry's major functional areas is listed, *except* marketing. Why? Either it is believed that electronics holds no revolutionary potential for petroleum marketing (which is palpably wrong), or the editors forgot to discuss marketing (which is more likely, and illustrates its stepchild status).

The order in which the four functional areas are listed also betrays the alienation of the oil industry from the consumer. The industry is implicitly defined as beginning with the search for oil and ending with its distribution from the refinery. But the truth is, it seems to me, that the industry begins with the needs of the customer for its products. From that primal position its definition moves steadily backstream to areas of progressively lesser importance, until it finally comes to rest at the "search for oil."

Beginning & end: The view that an industry is a customer-satisfying process, not a goods-producing process, is vital for all businessmen to understand. An industry begins with the customer and his needs, not with a patent, a raw material, or a selling skill. Given the customer's needs, the industry develops backwards, first concerning itself with the physical *delivery* of customer satisfactions. Then it moves back further to *creating* the things by which these satisfactions are in part achieved. How these materials are created is a matter of indifference to the customer, hence the particular form of manufacturing, processing, or what-have-you cannot be considered as a vital aspect of the industry. Finally, the industry moves back still further to *finding* the raw materials necessary for making its products.

The irony of some industries oriented toward technical research and development is that the scientists who occupy the high executive positions are totally unscientific when it comes to defining their companies' overall needs and purposes. They violate the first two rules of the scientific method —being aware of and defining their companies' problems, and then developing testable hypotheses about solving them. They are scientific only about the convenient things, such as laboratory and product experiments.

The reason that the customer (and the satisfaction of his deepest needs) is not considered as being "the problem" is not because there is any certain belief that no such problem exists, but because an organizational lifetime has conditioned management to look in the opposite direction. Marketing is a stepchild.

I do not mean that selling is ignored. Far from it. But selling, again, is not marketing. As already pointed out, selling concerns itself with the tricks and techniques of getting people to exchange their cash for your product. It is not concerned with the values that the exchange is all about. And it does not, as marketing invariably does, view the entire business process as consisting of a tightly integrated effort to discover, create, arouse, and satisfy customer needs. The customer is somebody "out there" who, with proper cunning, can be separated from his loose change.

Actually, not even selling gets much attention in some technologically minded firms. Because there is a virtually guaranteed market for the abundant flow of their new products, they do not actually know what a real market is. It is as if they lived in a planned economy, moving their products routinely from factory to retail outlet. Their successful concentration on products tends to convince them of the soundness of what they have been doing, and they fail to see the gathering clouds over the market.

Conclusion

Less than 75 years ago American railroads enjoyed a fierce loyalty among astute Wall Streeters. European monarchs invested in them heavily. Eternal wealth was thought to be the benediction for anybody who could scrape a few thousand dollars together to put into rail stocks. No other form of transportation could compete with the railroads in speed, flexibility, durability, economy, and growth potentials.

As Jacques Barzun put it, "By the turn of the century it was an institution, an image of man, a tradition, a code of honor, a source of poetry, a nursery of boyhood desires, a sublimest of toys, and the most solemn machine—next to the funeral hearse—that marks the epochs in man's life." [6]

Even after the advent of automobiles, trucks, and airplanes, the railroad tycoons remained imperturbably self-confident. If you had told them 60 years ago that in 30 years they would be flat on their backs, broke, and pleading for government subsidies, they would have thought you totally demented. Such a future was simply not considered possible. It was not even a discussable subject, or an askable question, or a matter which any sane person would consider worth speculating about. The very thought was insane. Yet a lot of insane notions now have matter-of-fact acceptance—for example, the idea of 100-ton tubes of metal moving smoothly through the air 20,000 feet above the earth, loaded with 100 sane and solid citizens casually drinking martinis—and they have dealt cruel blows to the railroads.

What specifically must other companies do to avoid this fate? What does customer orientation involve? These questions have in part been answered by the preceding examples and analysis. It would take another article to show in detail what is required for specific industries. In any case, it should be obvious that building an effective customer-oriented company involves far more than good intentions or promotional tricks; it involves profound matters of human organization and leadership. For the present, let me merely suggest what appear to be some general requirements.

Visceral feel of greatness: Obviously the company has to do what survival demands. It has to adapt to the requirements of the market, and it has to do it sooner rather than later. But mere survival is a so-so aspiration. Anybody can survive in some way or other, even the skid-row bum. The trick is to survive gallantly, to feel the surging impulse of commercial mastery; not just to experience the sweet smell of success, but to have the visceral feel of entrepreneurial greatness.

No organization can achieve greatness without a vigorous leader who is driven onward by his own pulsating *will to succeed.* He has to have a vision of grandeur, a vision that can produce eager followers in vast numbers. In business, the followers are the customers.

In order to produce these customers, the entire corporation must be viewed as a customer-creating and customer-satisfying organism. Management must think of itself not as producing products but as providing customer-creating value satisfactions. It must push this idea (and everything it means and requires) into every nook and cranny of the organization. It has to do this continuously and with the kind of flair that excites and stimulates the people in it. Otherwise, the company will be merely a series of pigeonholed parts, with no consolidating sense of purpose or direction.

In short, the organization must learn to think of itself not as producing goods or services but as *buying customers,* as doing the things that will make people *want* to do business with it. And the chief executive himself has the inescapable responsibility for creating this environment, this viewpoint, this attitude, this aspiration. He himself must set the company's style, its direction, and its goals. This means he has to know precisely where he himself wants to go, and to make sure the whole organization is enthusiastically aware of where that is. This is a first requisite of leadership, for *unless he knows where he is going, any road will take him there.*

If any road is okay, the chief executive might as well pack his attaché case and go fishing. If an organization does

6. Jacques Barzun, "Trains and the Mind of Man," *Holiday,* February 1960, p. 20.

not know or care where it is going, it does not need to advertise that fact with a ceremonial figurehead. Everybody will notice it soon enough.

Retrospective commentary

Amazed, finally, by his literary success, Isaac Bashevis Singer reconciled an attendant problem: "I think the moment you have published a book, it's not any more your private property. . . . If it has value, everybody can find in it what he finds, and I cannot tell the man I did not intend it to be so." Over the past 15 years, "Marketing Myopia" has become a case in point. Remarkably, the article spawned a legion of loyal partisans—not to mention a host of unlikely bedfellows.

Its most common and, I believe, most influential consequence is the way certain companies for the first time gave serious thought to the question of what businesses they are really in.

The strategic consequences of this have in many cases been dramatic. The best-known case, of course, is the shift in thinking of oneself as being in the "oil business" to being in the "energy business." In some instances the payoff has been spectacular (getting into coal, for example) and in others dreadful (in terms of the time and money spent so far on fuel cell research). Another successful example is a company with a large chain of retail shoe stores that redefined itself as a retailer of moderately priced, frequently purchased, widely assorted consumer specialty products. The result was a dramatic growth in volume, earnings, and return on assets.

Some companies, again for the first time, asked themselves whether they wished to be masters of certain technologies for which they would seek markets, or be masters of markets for which they would seek customer-satisfying products and services.

Choosing the former, one company has declared, in effect, "We are experts in glass technology. We intend to improve and expand that expertise with the object of creating products that will attract customers." This decision has forced the company into a much more systematic and customer-sensitive look at possible markets and users, even though its stated strategic object has been to capitalize on glass technology.

Deciding to concentrate on markets, another company has determined that "we want to help people (primarily women) enhance their beauty and sense of youthfulness." This company has expanded its line of cosmetic products, but has also entered the fields of proprietary drugs and vitamin supplements.

All these examples illustrate the "policy" results of "Marketing Myopia." On the operating level, there has been, I think, an extraordinary heightening of sensitivity to customers and consumers. R&D departments have cultivated a greater "external" orientation toward uses, users, and markets—balancing thereby the previously one-sided "internal" focus on materials and methods; upper management has realized that marketing and sales departments should be somewhat more willingly accommodated than before; finance departments have become more receptive to the legitimacy of budgets for market research and experimentation in marketing; and salesmen have been better trained to listen to and understand customer needs and problems, rather than merely to "push" the product.

A mirror, not a window

My impression is that the article has had more impact in industrial-products companies than in consumer-products companies—perhaps because the former had lagged most in customer orientation. There are at least two reasons for this lag: (1) industrial-products companies tend to be more capital intensive, and (2) in the past, at least, they have had to rely heavily on communicating face-to-face the technical character of what they made and sold. These points are worth explaining.

Capital-intensive businesses are understandably preoccupied with magnitudes, especially where the capital, once invested, cannot be easily moved, manipulated, or modified for the production of a variety of products—e.g., chemical plants, steel mills, airlines, and railroads. Understandably, they seek big volumes and operating efficiencies to pay off the equipment and meet the carrying costs.

At least one problem results: corporate power becomes disproportionately lodged with operating or financial executives. If you read the charter of one of the nation's largest companies, you will see that the chairman of the finance committee, not the chief executive officer, is the "chief." Executives with such backgrounds have an almost trained incapacity to see that getting "volume" may require understanding and serving many discrete and sometimes small market segments, rather than going after a perhaps mythical batch of big or homogeneous customers.

These executives also often fail to appreciate the competitive changes going on around them. They observe the changes, all right, but devalue their significance or underestimate their ability to nibble away at the company's markets.

Once dramatically alerted to the concept of segments, sectors, and customers, though, managers of capital-intensive businesses have become more responsive to the necessity of balancing their inescapable preoccupation with "paying the bills" or breaking even with the fact that the best way to accomplish this may be to pay more attention to segments, sectors, and customers.

The second reason industrial products companies have probably been more influenced by the article is that, in the case of the more technical industrial products or services, the necessity of clearly communicating product and service characteristics to prospects results in a lot of face-to-face "selling" effort. But precisely because the product is so complex, the situation produces salesmen who know the product more than they know the customer, who are more adept at explaining what they have and what it can do than learning what the customer's needs and problems are. The result has been a narrow product orientation rather than a liberating customer orientation, and "service" often suffered. To be sure, sellers said, "We have to provide service," but they tended to define service by looking into the mirror rather than out the window. They *thought* they were looking out the window at the customer, but it was actually a mirror—a reflection of their own product-oriented biases rather than a reflection of their customers' situations.

A manifesto, not a prescription

Not everything has been rosy. A lot of bizarre things have happened as a result of the article:

□
Some companies have developed what I call "marketing mania"—they've become obsessively responsive to every fleeting whim of the customer. Mass production operations have been converted to approximations of job shops, with cost and price consequences far exceeding the willingness of customers to buy the product.

□
Management has expanded product lines and added new lines of business without first establishing adequate control systems to run more complex operations.

□
Marketing staffs have suddenly and rapidly expanded themselves and their research budgets without either getting sufficient prior organizational support or, thereafter, producing sufficient results.

□
Companies that are functionally organized have converted to product, brand, or market-based organizations with the expectation of instant and miraculous results. The outcome has been ambiguity, frustration, confusion, corporate infighting, losses, and finally a reversion to functional arrangements that only worsened the situation.

□
Companies have attempted to "serve" customers by creating complex and beautifully efficient products or services that buyers are either too risk-averse to adopt or incapable of learning how to employ—in effect, there are now steam shovels for people who haven't yet learned to use spades. This problem has happened repeatedly in the so-called service industries (financial services, insurance, computer-based services) and with American companies selling in less-developed economies.

"Marketing Myopia" was not intended as analysis or even prescription; it was intended as manifesto. It did not pretend to take a balanced position. Nor was it a new idea—Peter F. Drucker, J.B. McKitterick, Wroe Alderson, John Howard, and Neil Borden had each done more original and balanced work on "the marketing concept." My scheme, however, tied marketing more closely to the inner orbit of business policy. Drucker—especially in *The Concept of the Corporation* and *The Practice of Management*—originally provided me with a great deal of insight.

My contribution, therefore, appears merely to have been a simple, brief, and useful way of communicating an existing way of thinking. I tried to do it in a very direct, but responsible, fashion, knowing that few readers (customers), especially managers and leaders, could stand much equivocation or hesitation. I also knew that the colorful and lightly documented affirmation works better than the tortuously reasoned explanation.

But why the enormous popularity of what was actually such a simple pre-existing idea? Why its appeal throughout the world to resolutely restrained scholars, implacably temperate managers, and high government officials, all accustomed to balanced and thoughtful calculation? Is it that concrete examples, joined to illustrate a simple idea and presented with some attention to literacy, communicate better than massive analytical reasoning that reads as though it were translated from the German? Is it that provocative assertions are more memorable and persuasive than restrained and balanced explanations, no matter who the audience? Is it that the character of the message is as much the message as its content? Or was mine not simply a different tune, but a new symphony? I don't know.

Of course, I'd do it again and in the same way, given my purposes, even with what more I now know—the good and the bad, the power of facts and the limits of rhetoric. If your mission is the moon, you don't use a car. Don Marquis's cockroach, Archy, provides some final consolation: "an idea is not responsible for who believes in it."

Reprint 75507

Changes that appeal to young customers may alienate older "core" customers. Does the company really have to start over?

The Case of the Migrating Markets

by Theodore Levitt

Theodore Levitt is the Edward W. Carter Professor of Business Administration at Harvard Business School and former editor of the Harvard Business Review.

HBR's cases are derived from the experiences of real companies and real people. As written, they are hypothetical, and the names used are fictitious.

DRAWINGS BY CHUCK MORRIS

July 1, 1990

Dear Bob,

Sorry to burden you, out there in Maine, in retirement. But how many mentors do I have? I still remember how, during my first week as your COO, you got to the heart of the Horst issue when you told the board: "Ladies and Gentlemen, companies don't sell drills, they sell holes." I need some of that sensibility just now.

Anybody would say things are fine at this company you put me in charge of. Profits are still growing comfortably and margins are good—not great, perhaps, but good. Our revenues climbed another notch last year, as they have every year since Steve was born (he's just finished his freshman year at Tech this spring, thank you very much). Conventional wisdom says nothing is wrong with us. We rank first in the industry. Wall Street loves us. The analysts love us. The board loves me (and not entirely for your sake). You probably saw that puff piece on us in the *Journal*, which called us "one of the few remaining American institutions."

The only report of problems is coming from my gut. Bob, most of what looks good is actually coming from price increases and incremental growth in the population at large. Our market shares aren't bad in the three core products, but these appeal to the most mature part of the population, which is going to decline but fast over the next 20 years. Our share in newer lines, directed toward younger people, is not acceptable. I'm uneasy about shifts in our customer base. Demographic trends are moving gradually against us. Who'll be our customers 20 years from now?

There are some fairly obvious things to do. My staff is already working on them—the "low risk" things. We could launch a program of "cognate" extensions, building on present brands and franchises with existing products or services. Birds Eye frozen vegetables launched Birds Eye frozen entrées, which launched Birds Eye frozen gourmet entrées. Look at Kodak getting into facsimile hardware, or Schlumberger with mineralization assessment in space. We could try to use our brand to get into new ventures more likely to impress younger people.

But is this really low risk? Is it not a five-foot leap over an eight-foot pit? We've always made great products, but we've also sold identity, trust, a touch of prestige. If we start expanding the lines and leveraging off the brand, especially in ways calculated to appeal to young people, won't we jeopardize our identity and customer loyalty? Have we not become hostages to our success with older core customers?

I want to do for my young hires what you did for me. I want this place to last. And yet I have a disturbing sense that we have to make ourselves over. Competitors are moving in from entirely different industries, not only with variations on our existing products but, more and more, with entirely different kinds of solutions that threaten our markets. I often feel like the CEO of a department store facing mass merchandisers, or a courier company fighting a fax machine. I see digital electronics transforming everything—even clothes and ditch digging (new ways to make holes, right?). Besides, even if we do things very gradually, we will almost certainly upset the financial community and the trade press and our employees. Why shake people up with changes and not go all the way?

I've asked some of our staff to think about this—"no holds barred." I told them even to think about selling off everything, starting from scratch: we'd keep our name for now—sacred, "an institution," better than gold. I told them to think of Coca-Cola announcing the elimination of its old formula. A kind of madness, wasn't it, but Coke came out smelling like a rose. What would it be like, I pressed them, if Philip Morris had sold all of *its* companies and brands and was left only with a pot of cash and some smart people to make it grow? By analogy, could we not buy back into related industries, here and in the Far East, but for a much lower price and with much more upside potential—and with none of the demographics against us? What would be left of S.S. Kresge if it hadn't transformed itself into K mart?

The problem may seem small now, but I fear that when it begins to grow it could quickly become a crisis. Why not cast the net of possibilities wider? I'm not too worried about the board because at least it will listen. Would you listen to a more radical proposal yourself? It's your life's work too. Let's talk when you've had a chance to digest this. My love to Kay.

As ever,

Philip

Should Philip build on his strengths or reinvent the "Great American Institution?"

Five experts consider Philip's alternatives.

Philip should look within the company for guidance – and create an entrepreneurial venture away from corporate headquarters.

I see many of the same challenges that are confronting the newspaper industry highlighted in Philip's company: changing demographic patterns, declining profits and margins, declining market share, price resistance, fierce competition, and, in an interesting way, a lack of entrepreneurial thinking.

Philip's letter struck me as nostalgic – kind of whiny, if you want the truth. While he should be applauded for thinking about these issues, it doesn't sound as if his heart is in it. Now it certainly is nice to ask the ex-leader for advice, but Philip should be speaking with the best and the brightest at his company, asking them how the company should move forward. He has to look within his own company and create an atmosphere and an environment where the employees are excited about the future.

Take Gannett, a $3.5 billion news and information corporation with

CATHLEEN BLACK is publisher of USA TODAY and executive vice president for marketing of Gannett Company, Inc.

37,000 employees. Almost ten years ago, now retired Gannett chairman, Al Neuharth, had a vision for *USA TODAY* – a massive and risky venture within a successful, established media company that was as healthy, if not more, than the company Philip describes. To carry out the project, a lot of enabling factors (such as advances in satellite technology) had to be in place, but what was really needed was someone who at the core of his being wanted to change and innovate.

If Philip's company is so tradition bound, then he should think about starting a new venture away from the company's heart. Fundamental change within any corporate culture is difficult; it's especially hard at a conservative company like Philip's. Let him create an entrepreneurial atmosphere that is not so close to the womb where everyone is second-guessing everyone. This allows the project leaders to forge new territory without all the overhead – literally and figuratively – of being next to corporate headquarters.

IBM took this path by sending a team to Boca Raton – far from the management structure in New York – to work on the personal computer. Likewise, at Gannett, which has operations in 40 of 50 states, the first two years of research for *USA TODAY* were conducted by a small independent team in Florida. Neuharth did not want the group to operate under the thumb of corporate nit-pickers. His message was "You go down there and figure out

how to do it. I will meet with you and discuss the problems and opportunities." And he did this, on a regular basis. In time, what the employees of the company learned and experienced was that *USA TODAY* was good for all of Gannett.

USA TODAY now serves as a laboratory for the entire company. And not just in news itself – but in marketing, advertising, systems, personnel, and circulation. It is a dynamic force from within for opportunity. We established a "loaner" program that rotates editors and reporters from throughout the company to *USA TODAY* for four months at a time.

This opportunity has been invigorating. The "loaners" are exposed to a different type of journalism in scope and style. They go back to their former jobs, or they go to others within the company with a broader sense of what the newspaper business is all about. This vision could be useful for Philip.

I believe that Philip needs to do two things:

☐ Line extensions are right if this is a conservative company. They don't fundamentally change the corporate character, they produce incremental revenue, and they invigorate people. If there are natural line extensions, Philip ought to create multidimensional, cross-departmental task forces with the charge to create new products that fit both the image and the quality reputation of the company. Philip need not necessarily sell off everything and start over. That seems to me throwing out the baby with the bathwater. That would be the easy course.

☐ The harder task is fundamental change for the corporation. If Philip really believes there is a product that fits the company, then he should proceed with it – but free it from what seems to be an institutional organization that rewards inertia over innovation. Philip needs to start moving beyond the prevailing corporate culture and start thinking like an entrepreneur. He should stop reminiscing about the past and move forward with spirit, determination, and speed.

Discipline yourself, Philip. Go back to the fundamentals. Plan your attack. And do it now.

DAVID W. JOHNSON *is president and chief executive officer of Campbell Soup Company. Prior to that, he was CEO of Gerber Products Company.*

Dear Philip:

Come on, Philip, you are better than "having a feeling in your gut." Fear drives us to extremes, and although I do not doubt your sincerity, there is a clear need for you to grasp this situation and apply some hard-nosed discipline.

Right now you are on top: number one in the marketplace, beloved by Wall Street and the board. You sit in the catbird seat. You have the money to bring in consultants or conduct research or take time off-site with your key executives or travel and immerse yourself in the marketplace with customers and competitors. What you need is a plan of attack to determine whether your instincts are valid or whether you are grabbing a handful of fog.

Philip, go back to the fundamentals of your training when you were COO. Think about how you can find out whether our great brands might be expanded to appeal to new groups of customers. One thing you and I know is this: change is constant. It is better to lead change than to react to change. In that context, leveraging and extending proven, high-quality, repeat-purchase brand names is al-ways preferred over launching a new name. Our brands make our asset bank. Consider using that source of power first. And the joy is that testing does not have to cost an arm and a leg. Take calculated risks.

I think your attitude toward young hires is dead on. As the leader of a great company, your job is to pass on the baton of leadership to a new group of runners. They must in turn have the chance to win versus competition and extend the life of their company beyond any mortal one. In a sense, we must give to our successors the secrets of eternal company life!

Watching the trends in other industries can be scary. But you should not feel like "a courier company fighting a fax machine." Remember, you are the leader. Your company knows more about its industry than any other. Don't sell yourself short. Rather, use the competitive adrenaline you feel to focus on how to throw existing and potential new competitors off guard. Lead with calculated innovation or insightful adaptation.

Toward the end of your letter, Philip, you crossed into the area of idealism. Rarely if ever can we clean the slate and start over. Selling off the company to get a pool of cash depends on a plan to drive extraordinary earnings, returns, and cash from a new orientation. Get the plan first. Think about how to make it happen. The Far East may be an opportunity. But first protect the home bases that have been won over the generations.

In conclusion, Philip, I would underline the following points:
□ Your position demands that you take the initiative and lead a new plan for the future.

□ If serious strategic planning had been a feature of the past two or three years, you would not have written me. That's a subject for another day!

Philip must plan his long-term strategy on markets rather than products.

Philip enjoys 20/20 foresight. He sees a demographic time bomb that has apparently escaped the notice of his colleagues, his board, industry analysts, Wall Street, and his competition. This kind of insight, in someone able to act on it, ought to be translatable into significant opportunity.

He must think through exactly what services are bundled into the products the company sells and then plan to grow the company by extending and building what it now provides so well.

Philip's most dramatic option, to sell and start anew with a "pot of cash and some smart people," is essentially a "buy low–sell high" strategy. It has some obvious drawbacks: he doesn't yet have a good idea about what to buy low after he sells high, and it sounds inconsistent with his desire to make "this place last." He ought to keep this option alive only as a counterpoint to more prosaic alternatives.

The company has an enviable roster of assets, including great products, decades of impressive financial

Act now, Philip. Our life's work must go forward, taking the shape and form as is necessary to reassert true leadership.

STEPHEN H. HAECKEL *is IBM's director of advance marketing development.*

performance, industry leadership, public admiration, a visionary CEO, and loyal customers. It also has time to deal with the decline of its traditional market in a noncrisis mode. Demographic forecasts are generally reliable, and a 20-year decline, even one as relatively steep as this, argues for a phase-out–phase-in, rather than a stop-start transformation.

Philip should consider an incremental approach – which permits extended milking of the company's cash cow to subsidize the discovery and development of new markets and inflicts minimum damage on the equities associated with being a "Great American Institution." The reputation of quality, leadership, and success that abide is an extraordinary asset, a competitive advantage more difficult to earn, perhaps, than any other. That said, the problem of winning a leadership position in new market segments remains.

As he sifts through his options, Philip should prioritize markets over products. Philip's "obvious things to do" are product centered. They involve tinkering with existing products and services to make them acceptable in markets they were not designed to address. Philip should do nothing to compromise his company's current leadership position, but he should begin, with some urgency, a systematic inventory of the assets that could be effectively leveraged in other than their traditional markets.

Twenty years of growth and profitability imply not only that the company has been successful in differ-

entiating itself but that it knows the source of that differentiation. That competitive advantage may come from a number of sources: the nature of the services wrapped around its products, the quality processes it employs, or the way it tailors specific combinations of products and services to individual customers. It may stem from infrastructure investments or from the quality of its channels. It could derive from superior information about its customers and competitors.

Underlying these kinds of differentiating values are more fundamental and generalized assets: the know-how required to create and manage the values that have differentiated the company, be they development, manufacturing, marketing, service, or financing values. Such intangible assets are just as real as capital assets. In particular, the creation and delivery of marketing and service values are becoming decisively important in many industries today, including high-tech, capital-intensive arenas such as IBM's. Solution, service, and market-driven strategies depend on such values.

No decision is more strategic than the selection of markets to be served. After know-how and value inventories have been made, Philip should match them against as wide a set of potentially attractive market segments as imagination and market research can provide. The company must be rigorous in determining what values are required for leadership in those markets and how these stack up against the assets Philip has or can reasonably acquire.

If good matches are not found, the Philip Morris alternative becomes compelling. If, however, good matches are found, Philip must begin shifting the center of gravity of the business from old markets to new, underwriting the process with profits thrown off by the traditional business. At this point, the issues of image and identity become crucial. Rather than trying to transfer brand equity, the company should focus on "logo equity" – make an "American Institution" contribute to the differentiation of new and newly branded products in customers' minds.

Your brand names are your company. Don't squander them.

Philip understands that he already owns the major solution to his problem: the company's strong brand equities. The way he must sustain and nurture his brand assets is to adapt his product lines to meet the changing needs of the marketplace – in this case, a growing number of younger people.

Today it is very expensive to launch new brand names – an option Philip unwisely appears to have under serious consideration. Defending or reinvigorating consumer goods brands is much easier than building them. Of all new products, 90% fail, while established brands, such as those Philip oversees, have long, profitable lives. Launching a new brand makes sense only if the new product is extremely desirable and very distinctive – an unusual combination in today's markets. Accordingly, Philip should be focusing on improving or rejuvenating his established brands rather than launching new ones – even where innovations are involved.

To sell off everything but retain the corporate brand name (or trademark) and attach it to totally new products would be an egregious mistake. Brand names have essential characteristics and associations in consumers' minds. A company's competence (and value) is often closely connected

CARL SPIELVOGEL *is chairman and chief executive officer of Backer Spielvogel Bates Worldwide, Inc., an international advertising agency.*

with its name – something that is not easily transferable for consumers. Any changes Philip contemplates must be within the realm of his company's perceived competence.

Philip would be well-advised to research what products the younger consumer market is seeking and then determine if the company has an associated competency. If so, Philip should design, develop, and launch the newly identified products. But he must make certain that the marketing communications he chooses for the new products involve clear distinctions between the established brands and the new ones.

It is highly unlikely that the markets that Philip's company targets are so inseparable that only older people will buy the established items while only younger people will be attracted to the newer products. Very few consumer products are used by one category of customers exclusively. Over a period of time, the buying public will not be noticeably concerned if Philip launches specialized extensions of his valuable brands that appeal to younger people. The sense of an "American Institution" will be preserved, as it should be.

It is unrealistic for a manufacturer of consumer items to worry about what will occur in the marketplace in 20 years. Philip should be concerned only about a time span equal to the outside lead time necessary to develop and launch a totally new product. Experience tells us this period should not be more than 5 to 7 years.

Managing change by extending brand names may temporarily cause concern among employees, the financial community, and the trade press, but these concerns should not alter a sound decision about future corporate direction. If the decision is correct and properly explained, employees will embrace it; the lasting effect of the trade press is minimal and should not be considered material; the financial community will reassess its own expectations.

Think globally, Philip. Leverage this American brand name into a valuable international asset.

Dear Philip:

It was good to hear from you, and I would really enjoy having the chance to talk over the issues raised in your letter. In the meantime, here are my first thoughts.

Go ahead with the "no holds barred" exercise. But don't spend too much time on it. First, possible buyers will be as aware of the demographic trends as you are and will guess why you might want to sell. The prices they offer will, therefore, take those trends into account and will reflect what they think they can make of the company. Their opportunities are equally open to us – but we should have the edge in making the most of them, thanks to our knowledge of the business.

More fundamentally, you could not buy back into related industries "for a much lower price and with

No one should fear change. The task is to manage it in an orderly, profitable fashion. Today's marketers must recognize what is occurring, analyze it, and make the necessary accommodations to get on with their business. These days, no one can stand still and be satisfied with the status quo.

SIR ADRIAN CADBURY, *now retired, is the former chairman of Cadbury Schweppes PLC.*

much more upside potential." Cheap, high-growth businesses are a pipe dream. I believe it is unrealistic to suppose that you can outsmart both the buyers of our company and the sellers of the businesses you want to buy.

As for the Philip Morris example, if it sold all its companies and brands, it would be left with a pot of cash, which the shareholders would understandably want returned to them. It would also be left with no smart people – they would have all gone off with the brands.

What concerns me about your Philip Morris example is that you may be thinking of the company – our company – as something separate from the brands that make it up and that have created its identity. This is to think like a banker – need I say more?

The company, its brands, and its identity are one; they are assets that will continue to grow in value, provided we keep investing in them. All else apart, it is becoming increasingly difficult to establish new brands and new identities – especially in international markets. Don't be afraid of leveraging our brands – look how Coca-Cola has used its brand to add value to goods outside the soft drinks market. Nor be afraid of replacing our existing

products and services with new ones that solve our customers' problems more effectively.

We must not underestimate the company's basic strengths. We are an institution and therefore we have a powerful base on which to build. We possess properties in our brands that are of great value. But like other forms of property, brands and identities must be defended against squatters, maintained in good repair, and modernized. We have consistently invested in our properties over the years and our shareholders expect us, in their interests, to develop them profitably – not to sell them off at sight value.

This brings me to what could be the greatest area of opportunity – the markets of the world. The company's brands and its reputation are recognized not only throughout the United States but in many other developed markets as well. The recognition of our name in many parts of the world is an asset waiting to be explored.

Before the strategy meeting of the board, why not take Alice on that overseas trip you have always promised her but have always been too busy to arrange? Include Japan and Western Europe in your itinerary, and get a firsthand feel for the way those markets are developing. Get to know Japan because the Pacific markets are the growth markets of the future; today's savers will in time become tomorrow's consumers. Get to know Western Europe as well. The population there is aging, and the section of the population that forms our mainstay in the United States is growing. European companies have been very quick to appreciate the many opportunities that an increasing number of elderly, reasonably well-off, retired people present.

Our core products have won the loyalty of mature citizens at home. We should repeat the success abroad. I am sure that you, the board, and our shareholders would rise to the challenge of turning an "American Institution" into an international one.

Let me know when we can meet.

Reprint 90408

▶ *To convert a tantalizing concept*
into a managerial instrument
of competitive power —

EXPLOIT the
Product Life Cycle

By Theodore Levitt

Most alert and thoughtful senior marketing executives are by now familiar with the concept of the product life cycle. Even a handful of uniquely cosmopolitan and up-to-date corporate presidents have familiarized themselves with this tantalizing concept. Yet a recent survey I took of such executives found none who used the concept in any strategic way whatever, and pitifully few who used it in any kind of tactical way. It has remained — as have so many fascinating theories in economics, physics, and sex — a remarkably durable but almost totally unemployed and seemingly unemployable piece of professional baggage whose presence in the rhetoric of professional discussions adds a much coveted but apparently unattainable legitimacy to the idea that marketing management is somehow a profession. There is, furthermore, a persistent feeling that the life cycle concept adds luster and believability to the insistent claim in certain circles that marketing is close to being some sort of science.[1]

The concept of the product life cycle is today at about the stage that the Copernican view of the universe was 300 years ago: a lot of people knew about it, but hardly anybody seemed to use it in any effective or productive way.

Now that so many people know and in some

AUTHOR'S NOTE: This article will appear in a forthcoming book, *Marketing Vision*, edited by Lee Adler.
[1] For discussions of the scientific claims or potentials of marketing, see George Schwartz, *Development of Marketing Theory* (Cincinnati, Ohio, South-Western Publishing Co., 1963); and Reavis Cox, Wroe Alderson, and Stanley J. Shapiro, editors, *Theory in Marketing* (Homewood, Illinois, Richard D. Irwin, Inc., Second Series, 1964).

fashion understand the product life cycle, it seems time to put it to work. The object of this article is to suggest some ways of using the concept effectively and of turning the knowledge of its existence into a managerial instrument of competitive power.

Since the concept has been presented somewhat differently by different authors and for different audiences, it is useful to review it briefly here so that every reader has the same background for the discussion which follows later in this article.

Historical Pattern

The life story of most successful products is a history of their passing through certain recognizable stages. These are shown in EXHIBIT I and occur in the following order:

Stage 1. Market Development — This is when a new product is first brought to market, before there is a proved demand for it, and often before it has been fully proved out technically in all respects. Sales are low and creep along slowly.

Stage 2. Market Growth — Demand begins to accelerate and the size of the total market expands rapidly. It might also be called the "Takeoff Stage."

Stage 3. Market Maturity — Demand levels off and grows, for the most part, only at the replacement and new family-formation rate.

Stage 4. Market Decline — The product begins to lose consumer appeal and sales drift downward, such as when buggy whips lost out with the advent of automobiles and when silk lost out to nylon.

Three operating questions will quickly occur to the alert executive:

EXHIBIT I. PRODUCT LIFE CYCLE — ENTIRE INDUSTRY

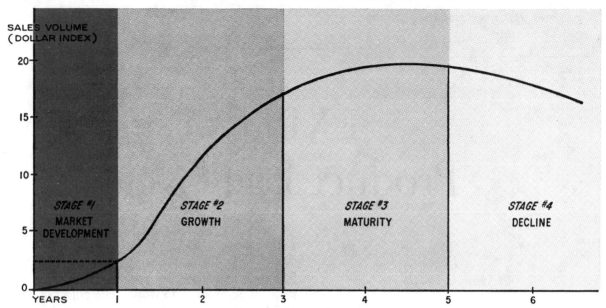

• Given a proposed new product or service, how and to what extent can the shape and duration of each stage be predicted?

• Given an existing product, how can one determine what stage it is in?

• Given all this knowledge, how can it be effectively used?

A brief further elaboration of each stage will be useful before dealing with these questions in detail.

Development Stage

Bringing a new product to market is fraught with unknowns, uncertainties, and frequently unknowable risks. Generally, demand has to be "created" during the product's initial *market development stage*. How long this takes depends on the product's complexity, its degree of newness, its fit into consumer needs, and the presence of competitive substitutes of one form or another. A proved cancer cure would require virtually no market development; it would get immediate massive support. An alleged superior substitute for the lost-wax process of sculpture casting would take lots longer.

While it has been demonstrated time after time that properly customer-oriented new product development is one of the primary conditions of sales and profit growth, what have been demonstrated even more conclusively are the ravaging costs and frequent fatalities associated with launching new products. Nothing seems to take more time, cost more money, involve more pitfalls, cause more anguish, or break more careers than do sincere and well-conceived new product programs. The fact is, most new products don't have any sort of classical life cycle curve at all. They have instead from the very outset an infinitely descending curve. The product not only doesn't get off the ground; it goes quickly under ground — six feet under.

It is little wonder, therefore, that some disillusioned and badly burned companies have recently adopted a more conservative policy — what I call the "used apple policy." Instead of aspiring to be the first company to see and seize an opportunity, they systematically avoid being first. They let others take the first bite of the supposedly juicy apple that tantalizes them. They let others do the pioneering. If the idea works, they quickly follow suit. They say, in effect, "The trouble with being a pioneer is that the pioneers get killed by the Indians." Hence, they say (thoroughly mixing their metaphors), "We don't have to get the first bite of the apple. The second one is good enough." They are willing to eat off a used apple, but they try to be alert enough to make sure it is only slightly used — that they at least get the second big bite, not the tenth skimpy one.

Growth Stage

The usual characteristic of a successful new product is a gradual rise in its sales curve during the market development stage. At some point in this rise a marked increase in consumer demand occurs and sales take off. The boom is on. This is the beginning of Stage 2 — the *market growth stage*. At this point potential competitors who have been watching developments during Stage 1 jump into the fray. The first ones to get in are generally those with an exceptionally effective "used apple policy." Some enter the market with carbon-copies of the originator's product. Others make functional and design improvements. And at this point product and brand differentiation begin to develop.

The ensuing fight for the consumer's patronage poses to the originating producer an entirely new set of problems. Instead of seeking ways of getting consumers to *try the product*, the originator now faces the more compelling problem of getting them to *prefer his brand*. This generally requires important changes in marketing strategies and methods. But the policies and tactics now adopted will be neither freely the sole choice of the originating producer, nor as experimental as they might have been during Stage 1. The presence of competitors both dictates and limits what can easily be tried — such as, for example, testing what is the best price level or the best channel of distribution.

As the rate of consumer acceptance accelerates, it generally becomes increasingly easy to open new distribution channels and retail outlets. The consequent filling of distribution pipelines generally causes the entire industry's factory sales to rise more rapidly than store sales. This creates an exaggerated impression of profit opportunity which, in turn, attracts more competitors. Some of these will begin to charge lower prices because of later advances in technology, production shortcuts, the need to take lower margins in order to get distribution, and the like. All this in time inescapably moves the industry to the threshold of a new stage of competition.

Maturity Stage

This new stage is the *market maturity stage*. The first sign of its advent is evidence of market saturation. This means that most consumer companies or households that are sales prospects will be owning or using the product. Sales now grow about on a par with population. No more distribution pipelines need be filled. Price competition now becomes intense. Competitive attempts to achieve and hold brand preference

now involve making finer and finer differentiations in the product, in customer services, and in the promotional practices and claims made for the product.

Typically, the market maturity stage forces the producer to concentrate on holding his distribution outlets, retaining his shelf space, and, in the end, trying to secure even more intensive distribution. Whereas during the market development stage the originator depended heavily on the positive efforts of his retailers and distributors to help sell his product, retailers and distributors will now frequently have been reduced largely to being merchandise-displayers and order-takers. In the case of branded products in particular, the originator must now, more than ever, communicate directly with the consumer.

The market maturity stage typically calls for a new kind of emphasis on competing more effectively. The originator is increasingly forced to appeal to the consumer on the basis of price, marginal product differences, or both. Depending on the product, services and deals offered in connection with it are often the clearest and most effective forms of differentiation. Beyond these, there will be attempts to create and promote fine product distinctions through packaging and advertising, and to appeal to special market segments. The market maturity stage can be passed through rapidly, as in the case of most women's fashion fads, or it can persist for generations with per capita consumption neither rising nor falling, as in the case of such staples as men's shoes and industrial fasteners. Or maturity can persist, but in a state of gradual but steady per capita decline, as in the case of beer and steel.

Decline Stage

When market maturity tapers off and consequently comes to an end, the product enters Stage 4 — *market decline*. In all cases of maturity and decline the industry is transformed. Few companies are able to weather the competitive storm. As demand declines, the overcapacity that was already apparent during the period of maturity now becomes endemic. Some producers see the handwriting implacably on the wall but feel that with proper management and cunning they will be one of the survivors after the industry-wide deluge they so clearly foresee. To hasten their competitors' eclipse directly, or to frighten them into early voluntary withdrawal from the industry, they initiate a variety of aggressively depressive tactics, propose mergers or buy-outs, and generally engage in activities that make life thanklessly burdensome for all firms, and make death the inevitable consequence for most of them. A few companies do indeed weather the storm, sustaining life through the constant descent that now clearly characterizes the industry. Production gets concentrated into fewer hands. Prices and margins get depressed. Consumers get bored. The only cases where there is any relief from this boredom and gradual euthanasia are where styling and fashion play some constantly revivifying role.

Preplanning Importance

Knowing that the lives of successful products and services are generally characterized by something like the pattern illustrated in Exhibit i can become the basis for important life-giving policies and practices. One of the greatest values of the life cycle concept is for managers about to launch a new product. The first step for them is to try to foresee the profile of the proposed product's cycle.

As with so many things in business, and perhaps uniquely in marketing, it is almost impossible to make universally useful suggestions regarding how to manage one's affairs. It is certainly particularly difficult to provide widely useful advice on how to foresee or predict the slope and duration of a product's life. Indeed, it is precisely because so little specific day-to-day guidance is possible in anything, and because no checklist has ever by itself been very useful to anybody for very long, that business management will probably never be a science — always an art — and will pay exceptional rewards to managers with rare talent, enormous energy, iron nerve, great capacity for assuming responsibility and bearing accountability.

But this does not mean that useful efforts cannot or should not be made to try to foresee the slope and duration of a new product's life. Time spent in attempting this kind of foresight not only helps assure that a more rational approach is brought to product planning and merchandising; also, as will be shown later, it can help create valuable lead time for important strategic and tactical moves after the product is brought to market. Specifically, it can be a great help in developing an orderly series of competitive moves, in expanding or stretching

out the life of a product, in maintaining a clean product line, and in purposely phasing out dying and costly old products.[2]

Failure Possibilities . . .

As pointed out above, the length and slope of the market development stage depend on the product's complexity, its degree of newness, its fit into customer needs, and the presence of competitive substitutes.

The more unique or distinctive the newness of the product, the longer it generally takes to get it successfully off the ground. The world does not automatically beat a path to the man with the better mousetrap.[3] The world has to be told, coddled, enticed, romanced, and even bribed (as with, for example, coupons, samples, free application aids, and the like). When the product's newness is distinctive and the job it is designed to do is unique, the public will generally be less quick to perceive it as something it clearly needs or wants.

This makes life particularly difficult for the innovator. He will have more than the usual difficulties of identifying those characteristics of his product and those supporting communications themes or devices which imply value to the consumer. As a consequence, the more distinctive the newness, the greater the risk of failure resulting either from insufficient working capital to sustain a long and frustrating period of creating enough solvent customers to make the proposition pay, or from the inability to convince investors and bankers that they should put up more money.

In any particular situation the more people who will be involved in making a single purchasing decision for a new product, the more drawn out Stage i will be. Thus in the highly fragmented construction materials industry, for example, success takes an exceptionally long time to catch hold; and having once caught hold, it tends to hold tenaciously for a long time — often too long. On the other hand, fashion items clearly catch on fastest and last shortest. But because fashion is so powerful, recently some companies in what often seem the least fashion-

[2] See Philip Kotler, "Phasing Out Weak Products," HBR March–April 1965, p. 107.

[3] For perhaps the ultimate example of how the world does *not* beat such a path, see the example of the man who actually, and to his painful regret, made a "better" mousetrap, in John B. Matthews, Jr., R. D. Buzzell, Theodore Levitt, and Ronald E. Frank, *Marketing: An Introductory Analysis* (New York, McGraw-Hill Book Company, Inc., 1964), p. 4.

influenced of industries (machine tools, for example) have shortened the market development stage by introducing elements of design and packaging fashion to their products.

What factors tend to prolong the market development stage and therefore raise the risk of failure? The more complex the product, the more distinctive its newness, the less influenced by fashion, the greater the number of persons influencing a single buying decision, the more costly, and the greater the required shift in the customer's usual way of doing things — these are the conditions most likely to slow things up and create problems.

. . . vs. Success Chances

But problems also create opportunities to control the forces arrayed against new product success. For example, the newer the product, the more important it becomes for the customers to have a favorable first experience with it. Newness creates a certain special visibility for the product, with a certain number of people standing on the sidelines to see how the first customers get on with it. If their first experience is unfavorable in some crucial way, this may have repercussions far out of proportion to the actual extent of the underfulfillment of the customers' expectations. But a favorable first experience or application will, for the same reason, get a lot of disproportionately favorable publicity.

The possibility of exaggerated disillusionment with a poor first experience can raise vital questions regarding the appropriate channels of distribution for a new product. On the one hand, getting the product successfully launched may require having — as in the case of, say, the early days of home washing machines — many retailers who can give consumers considerable help in the product's correct utilization and thus help assure a favorable first experience for those buyers. On the other hand, channels that provide this kind of help (such as small neighborhood appliance stores in the case of washing machines) during the market development stage may not be the ones best able to merchandise the product most successfully later when help in creating and personally reassuring customers is less important than wide product distribution. To the extent that channel decisions during this first stage sacrifice some of the requirements of the market development stage to some of the requirements of later stages, the rate of the product's acceptance by consumers at the outset may be delayed.

In entering the market development stage, pricing decisions are often particularly hard for the producer to make. Should he set an initially high price to recoup his investment quickly — i.e., "skim the cream" — or should he set a low price to discourage potential competition — i.e., "exclusion"? The answer depends on the innovator's estimate of the probable length of the product's life cycle, the degree of patent protection the product is likely to enjoy, the amount of capital needed to get the product off the ground, the elasticity of demand during the early life of the product, and many other factors. The decision that is finally made may affect not just the rate at which the product catches on at the beginning, but even the duration of its total life. Thus some products that are priced too low at the outset (particularly fashion goods, such as the chemise, or sack, a few years ago) may catch on so quickly that they become short-lived fads. A slower rate of consumer acceptance might often extend their life cycles and raise the total profits they yield.

The actual slope, or rate of the growth stage, depends on some of the same things as does success or failure in Stage 1. But the extent to which patent exclusiveness can play a critical role is sometimes inexplicably forgotten. More frequently than one might offhand expect, holders of strong patent positions fail to recognize either the market-development virtue of making their patents available to competitors or the market-destroying possibilities of failing to control more effectively their competitors' use of such products.

Generally speaking, the more producers there are of a new product, the more effort goes into developing a market for it. The net result is very likely to be more rapid and steeper growth of the total market. The originator's market share may fall, but his total sales and profits may rise more rapidly. Certainly this has been the case in recent years of color television; RCA's eagerness to make its tubes available to competitors reflects its recognition of the power of numbers over the power of monopoly.

On the other hand, the failure to set and enforce appropriate quality standards in the early days of polystyrene and polyethylene drinking glasses and cups produced such sloppy, inferior goods that it took years to recover the consumer's confidence and revive the growth pattern.

But to try to see in advance what a product's growth pattern might be is not very useful if one fails to distinguish between the industry pattern and the pattern of the single firm — for its particular brand. The industry's cycle will almost certainly be different from the cycle of individual firms. Moreover, the life cycle of a given product may be different for different companies in the same industry at the same point in time, and it certainly affects different companies in the same industry differently.

Originator's Burdens

The company with most at stake is the original producer — the company that launches an entirely new product. This company generally bears most of the costs, the tribulations, and certainly the risks of developing both the product and the market.

Competitive Pressure

Once the innovator demonstrates during the market development stage that a solid demand exists, armies of imitators rush in to capitalize on and help create the boom that becomes the market growth, or takeoff, stage. As a result, while exceedingly rapid growth will now characterize the product's total demand, for the originating company its growth stage paradoxically now becomes truncated. It has to share the boom with new competitors. Hence the potential rate of acceleration of its own takeoff is diminished and, indeed, may actually fail to last as long as the industry's. This occurs not only because there are so many competitors, but, as we noted earlier, also because competitors often come in with product improvements and lower prices. While these developments generally help keep the market expanding, they greatly restrict the originating company's rate of growth and the length of its takeoff stage.

All this can be illustrated by comparing the curve in EXHIBIT II with that in EXHIBIT I, which shows the life cycle for a product. During Stage 1 in EXHIBIT I there is generally only one company — the originator — even though the whole exhibit represents the entire industry. In Stage 1 the originator is the entire industry. But by Stage 2 he shares the industry with many competitors. Hence, while EXHIBIT I is an industry curve, its Stage 1 represents only a single company's sales.

EXHIBIT II shows the life cycle of the orig-

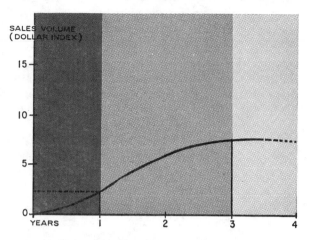

EXHIBIT II. PRODUCT LIFE CYCLE — ORIGINATING COMPANY

inator's brand — his own sales curve, not that of the industry. It can be seen that between Year 1 and Year 2 his sales are rising about as rapidly as the industry's. But after Year 2, while industry sales in EXHIBIT I are still in vigorous expansion, the originator's sales curve in EXHIBIT II has begun to slow its ascent. He is now sharing the boom with a great many competitors, some of whom are much better positioned now than he is.

Profit Squeeze

In the process the originator may begin to encounter a serious squeeze on his profit margins. EXHIBIT III, which traces the profits per unit of the originator's sales, illustrates this point. During the market development stage his per-unit profits are negative. Sales volume is too low at existing prices. However, during the

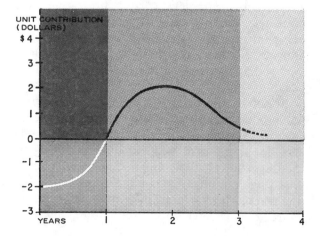

EXHIBIT III. UNIT PROFIT CONTRIBUTION LIFE CYCLE — ORIGINATING COMPANY

market growth stage unit profits boom as output rises and unit production costs fall. Total profits rise enormously. It is the presence of such lush profits that both attracts and ultimately destroys competitors.

Consequently, while (1) industry sales may still be rising nicely (as at the Year 3 point in EXHIBIT I), and (2) while the originating company's sales may at the same point of time have begun to slow down noticeably (as in EXHIBIT II), and (3) while at this point the originator's total profits may still be rising because his volume of sales is huge and on a slight upward trend, his profits per unit will often have taken a drastic downward course. Indeed, they will often have done so long before the sales curve flattened. They will have topped out and begun to decline perhaps around the Year 2 point (as in EXHIBIT III). By the time the originator's sales begin to flatten out (as at the Year 3 point in EXHIBIT II), unit profits may actually be approaching zero (as in EXHIBIT III).

At this point more competitors are in the industry, the rate of industry demand growth has slowed somewhat, and competitors are cutting prices. Some of them do this in order to get business, and others do it because their costs are lower owing to the fact that their equipment is more modern and productive.

The industry's Stage 3 — maturity — generally lasts as long as there are no important competitive substitutes (such as, for example, aluminum for steel in "tin" cans), no drastic shifts in influential value systems (such as the end of female modesty in the 1920's and the consequent destruction of the market for veils), no major changes in dominant fashions (such as the hour-glass female form and the end of waist cinchers), no changes in the demand for primary products which use the product in question (such as the effect of the decline of new railroad expansion on the demand for railroad ties), and no changes either in the rate of obsolescence of the product or in the character or introductory rate of product modifications.

Maturity can last for a long time, or it can actually never be attained. Fashion goods and fad items sometimes surge to sudden heights, hesitate momentarily at an uneasy peak, and then quickly drop off into total obscurity.

Stage Recognition

The various characteristics of the stages described above will help one to recognize the stage a particular product occupies at any given time. But hindsight will always be more accurate than current sight. Perhaps the best way of seeing one's current stage is to try to foresee the next stage and work backwards. This approach has several virtues:

❦ It forces one to look ahead, constantly to try to reforesee his future and competitive environment. This will have its own rewards. As Charles F. Kettering, perhaps the last of Detroit's primitive inventors and probably the greatest of all its inventors, was fond of saying, "We should all be concerned about the future because that's where we'll have to spend the rest of our lives." By looking at the future one can better assess the state of the present.

❦ Looking ahead gives more perspective to the present than looking at the present alone. Most people know more about the present than is good for them. It is neither healthy nor helpful to know the present too well, for our perception of the present is too often too heavily distorted by the urgent pressures of day-to-day events. To know where the present is in the continuum of competitive time and events, it often makes more sense to try to know what the future will bring, and when it will bring it, than to try to know what the present itself actually contains.

❦ Finally, the value of knowing what stage a product occupies at any given time resides only in the way that fact is used. But its use is always in the future. Hence a prediction of the future environment in which the information will be used is often more functional for the effective capitalization on knowledge about the present than knowledge about the present itself.

Sequential Actions

The life cycle concept can be effectively employed in the strategy of both existing and new products. For purposes of continuity and clarity, the remainder of this article will describe some of the uses of the concept from the early stages of new product planning through the later stages of keeping the product profitably alive. The chief discussion will focus on what I call a policy of "life extension" or "market stretching." [4]

To the extent that EXHIBITS II and III outline the classical patterns of successful new products,

[4] For related ideas on discerning opportunities for product revivification, see Lee Adler, "A New Orientation for Plotting a Marketing Strategy," *Business Horizons*, Winter 1964, p. 37.

one of the constant aims of the originating producer should be to avoid the severe discipline imposed by an early profit squeeze in the market growth stage, and to avoid the wear and waste so typical of the market maturity stage. Hence the following proposition would seem reasonable: when a company develops a new product or service, it should try to plan at the very outset a series of actions to be employed at various subsequent stages in the product's existence so that its sales and profit curves are constantly sustained rather than following their usual declining slope.

In other words, advance planning should be directed at extending, or stretching out, the life of the product. It is this idea of *planning in advance* of the actual launching of a new product to take specific actions later in its life cycle — actions designed to sustain its growth and profitability — which appears to have great potential as an instrument of long-term product strategy.

Nylon's Life

How this might work for a product can be illustrated by looking at the history of nylon.

The way in which nylon's booming sales life has been repeatedly and systematically extended and stretched can serve as a model for other products. What has happened in nylon may not have been purposely planned that way at the outset, but the results are quite as if they had been planned.

The first nylon end-uses were primarily military — parachutes, thread, rope. This was followed by nylon's entry into the circular knit market and its consequent domination of the women's hosiery business. Here it developed the kind of steadily rising growth and profit curves that every executive dreams about. After some years these curves began to flatten out. But before they flattened very noticeably, Du Pont had already developed measures designed to revitalize sales and profits. It did several things, each of which is demonstrated graphically in EXHIBIT IV. This exhibit and the explanation which follows take some liberties with the actual facts of the nylon situation in order to highlight the points I wish to make. But they take no liberties with the essential requisites of product strategy.

Point A of EXHIBIT IV shows the hypothetical

EXHIBIT IV. HYPOTHETICAL LIFE CYCLE — NYLON

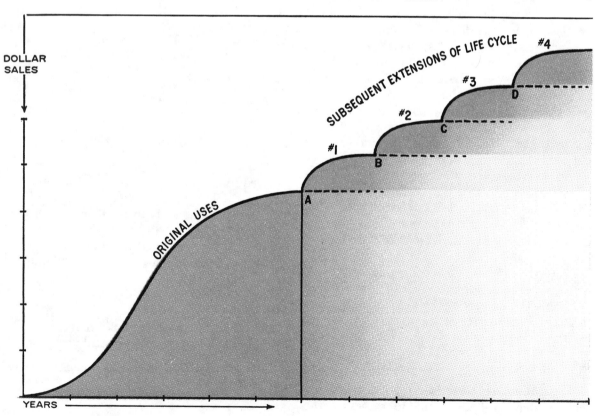

point at which the nylon curve (dominated at this point by hosiery) flattened out. If nothing further had been done, the sales curve would have continued along the flattened pace indicated by the dotted line at Point A. This is also the hypothetical point at which the first systematic effort was made to extend the product's life. Du Pont, in effect, took certain "actions" which pushed hosiery sales upward rather than continuing the path implied by the dotted line extension of the curve at Point A. At Point A action #1 pushed an otherwise flat curve upward.

At points B, C, and D still other new sales and profit expansion "actions" (#2, #3, #4, and so forth) were taken. What were these actions? Or, more usefully, what was their strategic content? What did they try to do? They involved strategies that tried to expand sales via four different routes:

1. Promoting more frequent usage of the product among current users.

2. Developing more varied usage of the product among current users.

3. Creating new users for the product by expanding the market.

4. Finding new uses for the basic material.

Frequent Usage. Du Pont studies had shown an increasing trend toward "bareleggedness" among women. This was coincident with the trend toward more casual living and a declining perception among teenagers of what might be called the "social necessity" of wearing stockings. In the light of those findings, one approach to propping up the flattening sales curves might have been to reiterate the social necessity of wearing stockings at all times. That would have been a sales-building action, though obviously difficult and exceedingly costly. But it could clearly have fulfilled the strategy of promoting more frequent usage among current users as a means of extending the product's life.

Varied Usage. For Du Pont, this strategy took the form of an attempt to promote the "fashion smartness" of tinted hose and later of patterned and highly textured hosiery. The idea was to raise each woman's inventory of hosiery by obsolescing the perception of hosiery as a fashion staple that came only in a narrow range of browns and pinks. Hosiery was to be converted from a "neutral" accessory to a central ingredient of fashion, with a "suitable" tint and

pattern for each outer garment in the lady's wardrobe.

This not only would raise sales by expanding women's hosiery wardrobes and stores' inventories, but would open the door for annual tint and pattern obsolescence much the same as there is an annual color obsolescence in outer garments. Beyond that, the use of color and pattern to focus attention on the leg would help arrest the decline of the leg as an element of sex appeal — a trend which some researchers had discerned and which, they claimed, damaged hosiery sales.

New Users. Creating new users for nylon hosiery might conceivably have taken the form of attempting to legitimize the necessity of wearing hosiery among early teenagers and subteenagers. Advertising, public relations, and merchandising of youthful social and style leaders would have been called for.

New Uses. For nylon, this tactic has had many triumphs — from varied types of hosiery, such as stretch stockings and stretch socks, to new uses, such as rugs, tires, bearings, and so forth. Indeed, if there had been no further product innovations designed to create new uses for nylon after the original military, miscellaneous, and circular knit uses, nylon consumption in 1962 would have reached a saturation level at approximately 50 million pounds annually.

Instead, in 1962 consumption exceeded 500 million pounds. Exhibit v demonstrates how the continuous development of new uses for the basic material constantly produced new waves of sales. The exhibit shows that in spite of the growth of the women's stocking market, the cumulative result of the military, circular knit, and miscellaneous grouping would have been a flattened sales curve by 1958. (Nylon's entry into the broadwoven market in 1944 substantially raised sales above what they would have been. Even so, the sales of broadwoven, circular knit, and military and miscellaneous groupings peaked in 1957.)

Had it not been for the addition of new uses for the same basic material — such as warp knits in 1945, tire cord in 1948, textured yarns in 1955, carpet yarns in 1959, and so forth — nylon would not have had the spectacularly rising consumption curve it has so clearly had. At various stages it would have exhausted its existing markets or been forced into decline by competing materials. The systematic search for

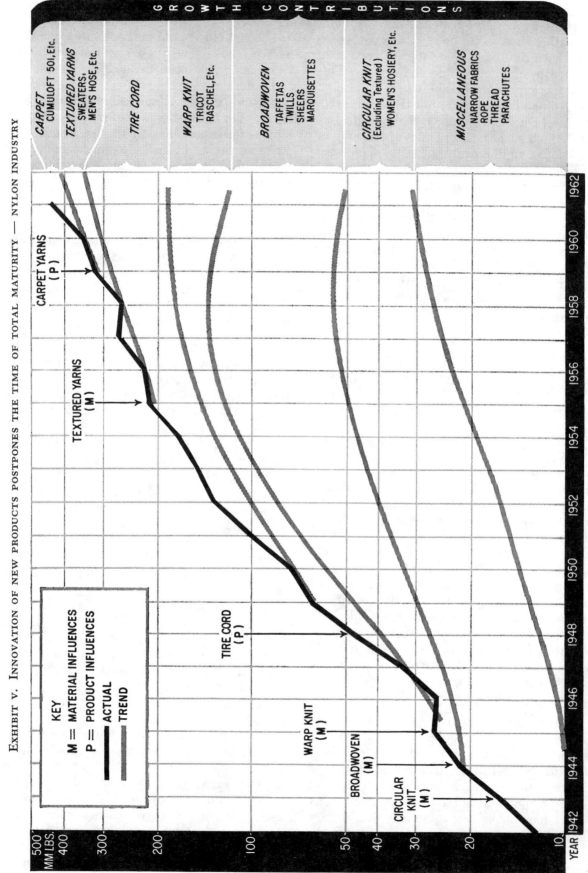

EXHIBIT V. INNOVATION OF NEW PRODUCTS POSTPONES THE TIME OF TOTAL MATURITY — NYLON INDUSTRY

Source: *Modern Textiles Magazine*, February 1964, p. 33. © 1962 by Jordan P. Yale.

new uses for the basic (and improved) material extended and stretched the product's life.

Other Examples

Few companies seem to employ in any systematic or planned way the four product life-stretching steps described above. Yet the successful application of this kind of stretching strategy has characterized the history of such well-known products as General Foods Corporation's "Jell-O" and Minnesota Mining & Manufacturing Co.'s "Scotch" tape.[5]

Jell-O was a pioneer in the easy-to-prepare gelatin dessert field. The soundness of the product concept and the excellence of its early marketing activities gave it beautifully ascending sales and profit curves almost from the start. But after some years these curves predictably began to flatten out. Scotch tape was also a pioneer product in its field. Once perfected, the product gained rapid market acceptance because of a sound product concept and an aggressive sales organization. But, again, in time the sales and profit curves began to flatten out. Before they flattened out very much, however, 3M, like General Foods, had already developed measures to sustain the early pace of sales and profits.

Both of these companies extended their products' lives by, in effect, doing all four of the things Du Pont did with nylon — creating more frequent usage among current users, more varied usage among current users, new users, and new uses for the basic "materials":

(1) The General Foods approach to increasing the frequency of serving Jell-O among current users was, essentially, to increase the number of flavors. From Don Wilson's famous "six delicious flavors," Jell-O moved up to over a dozen. On the other hand, 3M helped raise sales among its current users by developing a variety of handy Scotch tape dispensers which made the product easier to use.

(2) Creation of more varied usage of Jell-O among current dessert users involved its promotion as a base for salads and the facilitation of this usage by the development of a variety of vegetable flavored Jell-O's. Similarly, 3M developed a line of colored, patterned, waterproof, invisible, and write-on Scotch tapes which have enjoyed considerable success as sealing and decorating items for holiday and gift wrapping.

(3) Jell-O sought to create new users by pinpointing people who could not accept Jell-O as a popular dessert or salad product. Hence during the Metrecal boom Jell-O employed an advertising theme that successfully affixed to the product a fashion-oriented weight control appeal. Similarly, 3M introduced "Rocket" tape, a product much like Scotch tape but lower in price, and also developed a line of commercial cellophane tapes of various widths, lengths, and strengths. These actions broadened product use in commercial and industrial markets.

(4) Both Jell-O and 3M have sought out new uses for the basic material. It is known, for example, that women consumers use powdered gelatin dissolved in liquids as a means of strengthening their fingernails. Both men and women use it in the same way as a bone-building agent. Hence Jell-O introduced a "completely flavorless" Jell-O for just these purposes. 3M has also developed new uses for the basic material — from "double-coated" tape (adhesive on both sides) which competes with ordinary liquid adhesives, to the reflecting tape which festoons countless automobile bumpers, to marker strips which compete with paint.

Extension Strategies

The existence of the kinds of product life cycles illustrated in EXHIBITS I and II and the unit profit cycle in EXHIBIT III suggests that there may be considerable value for people involved in new product work to begin planning for the extension of the lives of their products even before these products are formally launched. To plan for new life-extending infusions of effort (as in EXHIBIT IV) at this pre-introduction stage can be extremely useful in three profoundly important ways.

1. *It generates an active rather than a reactive product policy.*

It systematically structures a company's long-term marketing and product development efforts in advance, rather than each effort or activity being merely a stop-gap response to the urgent pressures of repeated competitive thrusts and declining profits. The life-extension view of product policy enforces thinking and planning ahead — thinking in some systematic way about the moves likely to be made by potential competitors, about possible changes in consumer reactions to the product, and the required selling activities which best take advantage of these conditional events.

2. *It lays out a long-term plan designed to infuse new life into the product at the right*

[5] I am indebted to my colleague, Dr. Derek A. Newton, for these examples and other helpful suggestions.

time, with the right degree of care, and with the right amount of effort.

Many activities designed to raise the sales and profits of existing products or materials are often undertaken without regard to their relationship to each other or to timing — the optimum point of consumer readiness for such activities or the point of optimum competitive effectiveness. Careful advance planning, long before the need for such activity arises, can help assure that the timing, the care, and the efforts are appropriate to the situation.

For example, it appears extremely doubtful that the boom in women's hair coloring and hair tinting products would have been as spectacular if vigorous efforts to sell these products had preceded the boom in hair sprays and chemical hair fixers. The latter helped create a powerful consumer consciousness of hair fashions because they made it relatively easy to create and wear fashionable hair styles. Once it became easy for women to have fashionable hair styles, the resulting fashion consciousness helped open the door for hair colors and tints. It could not have happened the other way around, with colors and tints first creating fashion consciousness and thus raising the sales of sprays and fixers. Because understanding the reason for this precise order of events is essential for appreciating the importance of early pre-introduction life-extension planning, it is useful to go into a bit of detail. Consider:

For women, setting their hair has been a perennial problem for centuries. First, the length and treatment of their hair is one of the most obvious ways in which they distinguish themselves from men. Hence to be attractive in that distinction becomes crucial. Second, hair frames and highlights the face, much like an attractive wooden border frames and highlights a beautiful painting. Thus hair styling is an important element in accentuating the appearance of a woman's facial features. Third, since the hair is long and soft, it is hard to hold in an attractive arrangement. It gets mussed in sleep, wind, damp weather, sporting activities, and so forth.

Therefore, the effective *arrangement* of a woman's hair is understandably her first priority in hair care. An unkempt brunette would gain nothing from making herself into a blond. Indeed, in a country where blonds are in the minority, the switch from being an unkempt brunette to being an unkempt blond would simply draw attention to her sloppiness. But once the problem of arrangement became easily "solved" by sprays and fixers,

colors and tints could become big business, especially among women whose hair was beginning to turn gray.

The same order of priorities applies in industrial products. For example, it seems quite inconceivable that many manufacturing plants would easily have accepted the replacement of the old single-spindle, constantly man-tended screw machine by a computerized tape-tended, multiple-spindle machine. The mechanical tending of the multiple-spindle machine was a necessary intermediate step, if for no other reason than that it required a lesser work-flow change, and certainly a lesser conceptual leap for the companies and the machine-tending workers involved.

For Jell-O, it is unlikely that vegetable flavors would have been very successful before the idea of gelatin as a salad base had been pretty well accepted. Similarly, the promotion of colored and patterned Scotch tape as a gift and decorative seal might not have been as successful if department stores had not, as the result of their drive to compete more effectively with mass merchandisers by offering more customer services, previously demonstrated to the consumer what could be done to wrap and decorate gifts.

3. *Perhaps the most important benefit of engaging in advance, pre-introduction planning for sales-extending, market-stretching activities later in the product's life is that this practice forces a company to adopt a wider view of the nature of the product it is dealing with.*

Indeed, it may even force the adoption of a wider view of the company's business. Take the case of Jell-O. What is its product? Over the years Jell-O has become the brand umbrella for a wide range of dessert products, including cornstarch-base puddings, pie fillings, and the new "Whip'n Chill," a light dessert product similar to a Bavarian Creme or French Mousse. On the basis of these products, it might be said that the Jell-O Division of General Foods is in the "dessert technology" business.

In the case of tape, perhaps 3M has gone even further in this technological approach to its business. It has a particular expertise (technology) on which it has built a constantly expanding business. This expertise can be said to be that of bonding things (adhesives in the case of Scotch tape) to other things, particularly to thin materials. Hence we see 3M developing scores of profitable items, including electronic recording tape (bonding electron-sensitive materials to tape), and "Thermo-Fax" duplicating equipment and supplies (bonding heat reactive materials to paper).

Conclusion

For companies interested in continued growth and profits, successful new product strategy should be viewed as a planned totality that looks ahead over some years. For its own good, new product strategy should try to predict in some measure the likelihood, character, and timing of competitive and market events. While prediction is always hazardous and seldom very accurate, it is undoubtedly far better than not trying to predict at all. In fact, every product strategy and every business decision inescapably involves making a prediction about the future, about the market, and about competitors. To be more systematically aware of the predictions one is making so that one acts on them in an offensive rather than a defensive or reactive fashion — this is the real virtue of preplanning for market stretching and product life extension. The result will be a product strategy that includes some sort of *plan for a timed sequence of conditional moves.*

Even before entering the market development stage, the originator should make a judgment regarding the probable length of the product's normal life, taking into account the possibilities of expanding its uses and users. This judgment will also help determine many things — for example, whether to price the product on a skimming or a penetration basis, or what kind of relationship the company should develop with its resellers.

These considerations are important because at each stage in a product's life cycle each management decision must consider the competitive requirements of the next stage. Thus a decision to establish a strong branding policy during the market growth stage might help to insulate the brand against strong price competition later; a decision to establish a policy of "protected" dealers in the market development stage might facilitate point-of-sale promotions during the market growth state, and so on. In short, having a clear idea of future product development possibilities and market development opportunities should reduce the likelihood of becoming locked into forms of merchandising that might possibly prove undesirable.

This kind of advance thinking about new product strategy helps management avoid other pitfalls. For instance, advertising campaigns that look successful from a short-term view may hurt in the next stage of the life cycle. Thus at the outset Metrecal advertising used a strong medical theme. Sales boomed until imitative competitors successfully emphasized fashionable slimness. Metrecal had projected itself as the dietary for the overweight consumer, an image that proved far less appealing than that of being the dietary for people who were fashion-smart. But Metrecal's original appeal had been so strong and so well made that it was a formidable task later on to change people's impressions about the product. Obviously, with more careful long-range planning at the outset, a product's image can be more carefully positioned and advertising can have more clearly defined objectives.

Recognizing the importance of an orderly series of steps in the introduction of sales-building "actions" for new products should be a central ingredient of long-term product planning. A carefully preplanned program for market expansion, even before a new product is introduced, can have powerful virtues. The establishment of a rational plan for the future can also help to guide the direction and pace of the on-going technical research in support of the product. Although departures from such a plan will surely have to be made to accommodate unexpected events and revised judgments, the plan puts the company in a better position to *make* things happen rather than constantly having to react to things that *are* happening.

It is important that the originator does *not* delay this long-term planning until after the product's introduction. How the product should be introduced and the many uses for which it might be promoted at the outset should be a function of a careful consideration of the optimum sequence of suggested product appeals and product uses. Consideration must focus not just on optimum things to do, but as importantly on their optimum *sequence* — for instance, what the order of use of various appeals should be and what the order of suggested product uses should be. If Jell-O's first suggested use had been as a diet food, its chances of later making a big and easy impact in the gelatin dessert market undoubtedly would have been greatly diminished.

Similarly, if nylon hosiery had been promoted at the outset as a functional daytime-wear hosiery, its ability to replace silk as the acceptable high-fashion hosiery would have been greatly diminished.

To illustrate the virtue of pre-introduction planning for a product's later life, suppose a company has developed a nonpatentable new product — say, an ordinary kitchen salt shaker. Suppose that nobody now has any kind of shaker. One might say, before launching it, that (1) it has a potential market of "x" million household, institutional, and commercial consumers, (2) in two years market maturity will set in, and (3) in one year profit margins will fall because of the entry of competition. Hence one might lay out the following plan:

I. *End of first year: expand market among current users*
   Ideas — new designs, such as sterling shaker for formal use, "masculine" shaker for barbecue use, antique shaker for "Early American" households, miniature shaker for each table place setting, moisture-proof design for beach picnics.

II. *End of second year: expand market to new users*
   Ideas — designs for children, quaffer design for beer drinkers in bars, design for sadists to rub salt into open wounds.

III. *End of third year: find new uses*
   Ideas — make identical product for use as a pepper shaker, as decorative garlic salt shaker, shaker for household scouring powder, shaker to sprinkle silicon dust on parts being machined in machine shops, and so forth.

This effort to prethink methods of reactivating a flattening sales curve far in advance of its becoming flat enables product planners to assign priorities to each task, and to plan future production expansion and capital and marketing requirements in a systematic fashion. It prevents one's trying to do too many things at once, results in priorities being determined rationally instead of as accidental consequences of the timing of new ideas, and disciplines both the product development effort that is launched in support of a product's growth and the marketing effort that is required for its continued success.

Reprint 65608

Global Marketing

The globalization of markets

*Companies must learn
to operate
as if the world were
one large market—
ignoring superficial regional and
national differences*

Theodore Levitt

Many companies have become disillusioned with sales in the international marketplace as old markets become saturated and new ones must be found. How can they customize products for the demands of new markets? Which items will consumers want? With wily international competitors breathing down their necks, many organizations think that the game just isn't worth the effort.

In this powerful essay, the author asserts that well-managed companies have moved from emphasis on customizing items to offering globally standardized products that are advanced, functional, reliable— and low priced. Multinational companies that concentrated on idiosyncratic consumer preferences have become befuddled and unable to take in the forest because of the trees. Only global companies will achieve long-term success by concentrating on what everyone wants rather than worrying about the details of what everyone thinks they might like.

Mr. Levitt is Edward W. Carter Professor of Business Administration and head of the marketing area at the Harvard Business School. This is Mr. Levitt's twenty-third article for HBR; his classic "Marketing Myopia," first published in 1960, was reprinted in September-October 1975, and his last article was "Marketing Intangible Products and Product Intangibles" (May-June 1981).

Illustration by Karen Watson.

A powerful force drives the world toward a converging commonality, and that force is technology. It has proletarianized communication, transport, and travel. It has made isolated places and impoverished peoples eager for modernity's allurements. Almost everyone everywhere wants all the things they have heard about, seen, or experienced via the new technologies.

The result is a new commercial reality— the emergence of global markets for standardized consumer products on a previously unimagined scale of magnitude. Corporations geared to this new reality benefit from enormous economies of scale in production, distribution, marketing, and management. By translating these benefits into reduced world prices, they can decimate competitors that still live in the disabling grip of old assumptions about how the world works.

Gone are accustomed differences in national or regional preference. Gone are the days when a company could sell last year's models—or lesser versions of advanced products—in the less-developed world. And gone are the days when prices, margins, and profits abroad were generally higher than at home.

The globalization of markets is at hand. With that, the multinational commercial world nears its end, and so does the multinational corporation.

The multinational and the global corporation are not the same thing. The multinational corporation operates in a number of countries, and adjusts its products and practices in each—at high relative costs. The global corporation operates with resolute constancy—at low relative cost—as if the entire world

---

1 In a landmark article, Robert D. Buzzell pointed out the rapidity with which barriers to standardization were falling. In all cases they succumbed to more and cheaper advanced ways of doing things. See "Can You Standardize Multinational Marketing?" HBR November-December 1968, p. 102.

(or major regions of it) were a single entity; it sells the same things in the same way everywhere.

Which strategy is better is not a matter of opinion but of necessity. Worldwide communications carry everywhere the constant drumbeat of modern possibilities to lighten and enhance work, raise living standards, divert, and entertain. The same countries that ask the world to recognize and respect the individuality of their cultures insist on the wholesale transfer to them of modern goods, services, and technologies. Modernity is not just a wish but also a widespread practice among those who cling, with unyielding passion or religious fervor, to ancient attitudes and heritages.

Who can forget the televised scenes during the 1979 Iranian uprisings of young men in fashionable French-cut trousers and silky body shirts thirsting with raised modern weapons for blood in the name of Islamic fundamentalism?

In Brazil, thousands swarm daily from pre-industrial Bahian darkness into exploding coastal cities, there quickly to install television sets in crowded corrugated huts and, next to battered Volkswagens, make sacrificial offerings of fruit and fresh-killed chickens to Macumban spirits by candlelight.

During Biafra's fratricidal war against the Ibos, daily televised reports showed soldiers carrying bloodstained swords and listening to transistor radios while drinking Coca-Cola.

In the isolated Siberian city of Krasnoyarsk, with no paved streets and censored news, occasional Western travelers are stealthily propositioned for cigarettes, digital watches, and even the clothes off their backs.

The organized smuggling of electronic equipment, used automobiles, western clothing, cosmetics, and pirated movies into primitive places exceeds even the thriving underground trade in modern weapons and their military mercenaries.

A thousand suggestive ways attest to the ubiquity of the desire for the most advanced things that the world makes and sells—goods of the best quality and reliability at the lowest price. The world's needs and desires have been irrevocably homogenized. This makes the multinational corporation obsolete and the global corporation absolute.

Living in the Republic of Technology

Daniel J. Boorstin, author of the monumental trilogy *The Americans*, characterized our age as driven by "the Republic of Technology [whose] supreme law…is convergence, the tendency for everything to become more like everything else."

In business, this trend has pushed markets toward global commonality. Corporations sell standardized products in the same way everywhere—autos, steel, chemicals, petroleum, cement, agricultural commodities and equipment, industrial and commercial construction, banking and insurance services, computers, semiconductors, transport, electronic instruments, pharmaceuticals, and telecommunications, to mention some of the obvious.

Nor is the sweeping gale of globalization confined to these raw material or high-tech products, where the universal language of customers and users facilitates standardization. The transforming winds whipped up by the proletarianization of communication and travel enter every crevice of life.

Commercially, nothing confirms this as much as the success of McDonald's from the Champs Elysées to the Ginza, of Coca-Cola in Bahrain and Pepsi-Cola in Moscow, and of rock music, Greek salad, Hollywood movies, Revlon cosmetics, Sony televisions, and Levi jeans everywhere. "High-touch" products are as ubiquitous as high-tech.

Starting from opposing sides, the high-tech and the high-touch ends of the commercial spectrum gradually consume the undistributed middle in their cosmopolitan orbit. No one is exempt and nothing can stop the process. Everywhere everything gets more and more like everything else as the world's preference structure is relentlessly homogenized.

Consider the cases of Coca-Cola and Pepsi-Cola, which are globally standardized products sold everywhere and welcomed by everyone. Both successfully cross multitudes of national, regional, and ethnic taste buds trained to a variety of deeply ingrained local preferences of taste, flavor, consistency, effervescence, and aftertaste. Everywhere both sell well. Cigarettes, too, especially American-made, make year-to-year global inroads on territories previously held in the firm grip of other, mostly local, blends.

These are not exceptional examples. (Indeed their global reach would be even greater were it not for artificial trade barriers.) They exemplify a general drift toward the homogenization of the world and how companies distribute, finance, and price products.[1] Nothing is exempt. The products and methods of the industrialized world play a single tune for all the world, and all the world eagerly dances to it.

Ancient differences in national tastes or modes of doing business disappear. The commonality of preference leads inescapably to the standardization of products, manufacturing, and the institutions of trade and commerce. Small nation-based markets transmogrify and expand. Success in world competition turns on efficiency in production, distribution, marketing, and management, and inevitably becomes focused on price.

The most effective world competitors incorporate superior quality and reliability into their cost structures. They sell in all national markets the same kind of products sold at home or in their largest export market. They compete on the basis of appropriate value – the best combinations of price, quality, reliability, and delivery for products that are globally identical with respect to design, function, and even fashion.

That, and little else, explains the surging success of Japanese companies dealing worldwide in a vast variety of products – both tangible products like steel, cars, motorcyles, hi-fi equipment, farm machinery, robots, microprocessors, carbon fibers, and now even textiles, and intangibles like banking, shipping, general contracting, and soon computer software. Nor are high-quality and low-cost operations incompatible, as a host of consulting organizations and data engineers argue with vigorous vacuity. The reported data are incomplete, wrongly analyzed, and contradictory. The truth is that low-cost operations are the hallmark of corporate cultures that require and produce quality in all that they do. High quality and low costs are not opposing postures. They are compatible, twin identities of superior practice.[2]

To say that Japan's companies are not global because they export cars with left-side drives to the United States and the European continent, while those in Japan have right-side drives, or because they sell office machines through distributors in the United States but directly at home, or speak Portuguese in Brazil is to mistake a difference for a distinction. The same is true of Safeway and Southland retail chains operating effectively in the Middle East, and to not only native but also imported populations from Korea, the Philippines, Pakistan, India, Thailand, Britain, and the United States. National rules of the road differ, and so do distribution channels and languages. Japan's distinction is its unrelenting push for economy and value enhancement. That translates into a drive for standardization at high quality levels.

Vindication of the Model T

If a company forces costs and prices down and pushes quality and reliability up – while maintaining reasonable concern for suitability – customers will prefer its world-standardized products. The theory holds, at this stage in the evolution of globalization, no matter what conventional market research and even common sense may suggest about different national and regional tastes, preferences, needs, and institutions. The Japanese have repeatedly vindicated this theory, as did Henry Ford with the Model T. Most important, so have their imitators, including companies from South Korea (television sets and heavy construction), Malaysia (personal calculators and microcomputers), Brazil (auto parts and tools), Colombia (apparel), Singapore (optical equipment), and yes, even from the United States (office copiers, computers, bicycles, castings), Western Europe (automatic washing machines), Rumania (housewares), Hungary (apparel), Yugoslavia (furniture), and Israel (pagination equipment).

Of course, large companies operating in a single nation or even a single city don't standardize everything they make, sell, or do. They have product lines instead of a single product version, and multiple distribution channels. There are neighborhood, local, regional, ethnic, and institutional differences, even within metropolitan areas. But although companies customize products for particular market segments, they know that success in a world with homogenized demand requires a search for sales opportunities in similar segments across the globe in order to achieve the economies of scale necessary to compete.

Such a search works because a market segment in one country is seldom unique; it has close cousins everywhere precisely because technology has homogenized the globe. Even small local segments have their global equivalents everywhere and become subject to global competition, especially on price.

The global competitor will seek constantly to standardize his offering everywhere. He will digress from this standardization only after exhausting all possibilities to retain it, and he will push for reinstatement of standardization whenever digression and divergence have occurred. He will never assume that the customer is a king who knows his own wishes.

Trouble increasingly stalks companies that lack clarified global focus and remain inattentive to the economics of simplicity and standardization. The most endangered companies in the rapidly evolving world tend to be those that dominate rather small domestic markets with high value-added products for which there are smaller markets elsewhere. With transportation costs proportionately low, distant competitors will enter the now-sheltered markets of those companies with goods produced more cheaply under scale-efficient conditions. Global competition spells the end of domestic territoriality, no matter how diminutive the territory may be.

2 There is powerful new evidence for this, even though the opposite has been urged by analysts of PIMS data for nearly a decade. See "Product Quality: Cost Production and Business Performance – A Test of Some Key Hypotheses" by Lynn W. Phillips, Dae Chang, and Robert D. Buzzell, Harvard Business School Working Paper No. 83-13.

Economies of scope

One argument that opposes globalization says that flexible factory automation will enable plants of massive size to change products and product features quickly, without stopping the manufacturing process. These factories of the future could thus produce broad lines of customized products without sacrificing the scale economies that come from long production runs of standardized items. Computer-aided design and manufacturing (CAD/CAM), combined with robotics, will create a new equipment and process technology (EPT) that will make small plants located close to their markets as efficient as large ones located distantly. Economies of scale will not dominate, but rather economies of scope – the ability of either large or small plants to produce great varieties of relatively customized products at remarkably low costs. If that happens, customers will have no need to abandon special preferences.

I will not deny the power of these possibilities. But possibilities do not make probabilities. There is no conceivable way in which flexible factory automation can achieve the scale economies of a modernized plant dedicated to mass production of standardized lines. The new digitized equipment and process technologies are available to all. Manufacturers with minimal customization and narrow product-line breadth will have costs far below those with more customization and wider lines.

When the global producer offers his lower costs internationally, his patronage expands exponentially. He not only reaches into distant markets, but also attracts customers who previously held to local preferences and now capitulate to the attractions of lesser prices. The strategy of standardization not only responds to worldwide homogenized markets but also expands those markets with aggressive low pricing. The new technological juggernaut taps an ancient motivation – to make one's money go as far as possible. This is universal – not simply a motivation but actually a need.

The hedgehog knows

The difference between the hedgehog and the fox, wrote Sir Isaiah Berlin in distinguishing between Dostoevski and Tolstoy, is that the fox knows a lot about a great many things, but the hedgehog knows everything about one great thing. The multinational corporation knows a lot about a great many countries and congenially adapts to supposed differences. It willingly accepts vestigial national differences, not questioning the possibility of their transformation, not recognizing how the world is ready and eager for the benefit of modernity, especially when the price is right. The multinational corporation's accommodating mode to visible national differences is medieval.

By contrast, the global corporation knows everything about one great thing. It knows about the absolute need to be competitive on a worldwide basis as well as nationally and seeks constantly to drive down prices by standardizing what it sells and how it operates. It treats the world as composed of few standardized markets rather than many customized markets. It actively seeks and vigorously works toward global convergence. Its mission is modernity and its mode, price competition, even when it sells top-of-the-line, high-end products. It knows about the one great thing all nations and people have in common: scarcity.

Nobody takes scarcity lying down; everyone wants more. This in part explains division of labor and specialization of production. They enable people and nations to optimize their conditions through trade. The median is usually money.

Experience teaches that money has three special qualities: scarcity, difficulty of acquisition, and transience. People understandably treat it with respect. Everyone in the increasingly homogenized world market wants products and features that everybody else wants. If the price is low enough, they will take highly standardized world products, even if these aren't exactly what mother said was suitable, what immemorial custom decreed was right, or what market-research fabulists asserted was preferred.

The implacable truth of all modern production – whether of tangible or intangible goods – is that large-scale production of standardized items is generally cheaper within a wide range of volume than small-scale production. Some argue that CAD/CAM will allow companies to manufacture customized products on a small scale – but cheaply. But the argument misses the point. (For a more detailed discussion, see the insert, "Economies of scope.") If a company treats the world as one or two distinctive product markets, it can serve the world more economically than if it treats it as three, four, or five product markets.

Why remaining differences?

Different cultural preferences, national tastes and standards, and business institutions are vestiges of the past. Some inheritances die gradually; others prosper and expand into mainstream global preferences. So-called ethnic markets are a good example. Chinese food, pita bread, country and western music, pizza, and jazz are everywhere. They are market segments that exist in worldwide proportions. They don't deny or contradict global homogenization but confirm it.

Many of today's differences among nations as to products and their features actually reflect the respectful accommodation of multinational corporations to what they believe are fixed local preferences. They *believe* preferences are fixed, not because they are but because of rigid habits of thinking about what actually is. Most executives in multinational corporations are thoughtlessly accommodating. They falsely presume that marketing means giving the customer what he says he wants rather than trying to understand exactly what he'd like. So they persist with high-cost, customized multinational products and practices instead of pressing hard and pressing properly for global standardization.

I do not advocate the systematic disregard of local or national differences. But a company's sensitivity to such differences does not require that it ignore the possibilities of doing things differently or better.

There are, for example, enormous differences among Middle Eastern countries. Some are socialist, some monarchies, some republics. Some take their legal heritage from the Napoleonic Code, some from the Ottoman Empire, and some from the British common law; except for Israel, all are influenced by Islam. Doing business means personalizing the business relationship in an obsessively intimate fashion. During the month of Ramadan, business discussions can start only after 10 o'clock at night, when people are tired and full of food after a day of fasting. A company must almost certainly have a local partner; a local lawyer is required (as, say, in New York), and irrevocable letters of credit are essential. Yet, as Coca-Cola's Senior Vice President Sam Ayoub noted, "Arabs are much more capable of making distinctions between cultural and religious purposes on the one hand and economic realities on the other than is generally assumed. Islam is compatible with science and modern times."

Barriers to globalization are not confined to the Middle East. The free transfer of technology and data across the boundaries of the European Common Market countries are hampered by legal and financial impediments. And there is resistance to radio and television interference ("pollution") among neighboring European countries.

But the past is a good guide to the future. With persistence and appropriate means, barriers against superior technologies and economics have always fallen. There is no recorded exception where reasonable effort has been made to overcome them. It is very much a matter of time and effort.

A failure in global imagination

Many companies have tried to standardize world practice by exporting domestic products and processes without accommodation or change – and have failed miserably. Their deficiencies have been seized on as evidence of bovine stupidity in the face of abject impossibility. Advocates of global standardization see them as examples of failures in execution.

In fact, poor execution is often an important cause. More important, however, is failure of nerve – failure of imagination.

Consider the case for the introduction of fully automatic home laundry equipment in Western Europe at a time when few homes had even semi-automatic machines. Hoover, Ltd., whose parent company was headquartered in North Canton, Ohio had a prominent presence in Britain as a producer of vacuum cleaners and washing machines. Due to insufficient demand in the home market and low exports to the European continent, the large washing machine plant in England operated far below capacity. The company needed to sell more of its semiautomatic or automatic machines.

Because it had a "proper" marketing orientation, Hoover conducted consumer preference studies in Britain and each major continental country. The results showed feature preferences clearly enough among several countries (see the *Exhibit*).

The incremental unit variable costs (in pounds sterling) of customizing to meet just a few of the national preferences were:

	£	s.	d.
Stainless steel vs. enamel drum	1	0	0
Porthole window		10	0
Spin speed of 800 rpm vs. 700 rpm		15	0
Water heater	2	15	0
6 vs. 5 kilos capacity	1	10	0
	£ 6	10 s	0 d

$18.20 at the exchange rate of that time.

Considerable plant investment was needed to meet other preferences.

The lowest retail prices (in pounds sterling) of leading locally produced brands in the various countries were approximately:

U.K.	£110
France	114
West Germany	113
Sweden	134
Italy	57

Product customization in each country would have put Hoover in a poor competitive position on the basis of price, mostly due to the higher manufacturing costs incurred by short production runs for separate features. Because Common Market tariff reduction programs were then incomplete, Hoover also paid tariff duties in each continental country.

How to make a creative analysis

In the Hoover case, an imaginative analysis of automatic washing machine sales in each country would have revealed that:

1   Italian automatics, small in capacity and size, low-powered, without built-in heaters, with porcelain enamel tubs, were priced aggressively low and were gaining large market shares in all countries, including West Germany.

2   The best-selling automatics in West Germany were heavily advertised (three times more than the next most promoted brand), were ideally suited to national tastes, and were also by far the highest priced machines available in that country.

3   Italy, with the lowest penetration of washing machines of any kind (manual, semi-automatic, or automatic) was rapidly going directly to automatics, skipping the pattern of first buying hand-wringer, manually assisted machines and then semiautomatics.

4   Detergent manufacturers were just beginning to promote the technique of cold-water and tepid-water laundering then used in the United States.

The growing success of small, low-powered, low-speed, low-capacity, low-priced Italian machines, even against the preferred but highly priced and highly promoted brand in West Germany, was significant. It contained a powerful message that was lost on managers confidently wedded to a distorted version of the marketing concept according to which you give the customer what he says he wants. In fact the customers *said* they wanted certain features, but their behavior demonstrated they'd take other features provided the price and the promotion were right.

In this case it was obvious that, under prevailing conditions, people preferred a low-priced automatic over any kind of manual or semiautomatic machine and certainly over higher priced automatics, even though the low-priced automatics failed to fulfill all their expressed preferences. The supposedly meticulous and demanding German consumers violated all expectations by buying the simple, low-priced Italian machines.

It was equally clear that people were profoundly influenced by promotions of automatic washers; in West Germany, the most heavily promoted ideal machine also had the largest market share despite its high price. Two things clearly influenced customers to buy: low price regardless of feature preferences and heavy promotion regardless of price. Both factors helped homemakers get what they most wanted—the superior benefits bestowed by fully automatic machines.

Hoover should have aggressively sold a simple, standardized high-quality machine at a low price (afforded by the 17% variable cost reduction that the elimination of £6-10-0 worth of extra features made possible). The suggested retail prices could have been somewhat less than £100. The extra funds "saved" by avoiding unnecessary plant modifications would have supported an extended service network and aggressive media promotions.

Hoover's media message should have been: *this* is the machine that you, the homemaker, *deserve* to have to reduce the repetitive heavy daily household burdens, so that *you* may have more constructive time to spend with your children and your husband. The promotion should also have targeted the husband to give him, preferably in the presence of his wife, a sense of obligation to provide an automatic washer for her even before he bought an automobile for himself. An aggressively low price, combined with heavy promotion of this kind, would have overcome previously expressed preferences for particular features.

The Hoover case illustrates how the perverse practice of the marketing concept and the absence of any kind of marketing imagination let multinational attitudes survive when customers actually want the benefits of global standardization. The whole project got off on the wrong foot. It asked people what features they wanted in a washing machine rather than what they wanted out of life. Selling a line of products individually tailored to each nation is thoughtless. Managers who took pride in practicing the marketing concept to the fullest did not, in fact, practice it at all. Hoover asked the wrong questions, then applied neither thought nor imagination to the answers. Such companies are like the ethnocentricists

Exhibit	Consumer preferences as to automatic washing machine features in the 1960s				
Features	Great Britain	Italy	West Germany	France	Sweden
Shell dimensions*	34" and narrow	Low and narrow	34" and wide	34" and narrow	34" and wide
Drum material	Enamel	Enamel	Stainless steel	Enamel	Stainless steel
Loading	Top	Front	Front	Front	Front
Front porthole	Yes/no	Yes	Yes	Yes	Yes
Capacity	5 kilos	4 kilos	6 kilos	5 kilos	6 kilos
Spin speed	700 rpm	400 rpm	850 rpm	600 rpm	800 rpm
Water-heating system	No†	Yes	Yes††	Yes	No†
Washing action	Agitator	Tumble	Tumble	Agitator	Tumble
Styling features	Inconspicuous appearance	Brightly colored	Indestructible appearance	Elegant appearance	Strong appearance

*34" height was (in the process of being adopted as) a standard work-surface height in Europe.

†Most British and Swedish homes had centrally heated hot water.

††West Germans preferred to launder at temperatures higher than generally provided centrally.

in the Middle Ages who saw with everyday clarity the sun revolving around the earth and offered it as Truth. With no additional data but a more searching mind, Copernicus, like the hedgehog, interpreted a more compelling and accurate reality. Data do not yield information except with the intervention of the mind. Information does not yield meaning except with the intervention of imagination.

Accepting the inevitable

The global corporation accepts for better or for worse that technology drives consumers relentlessly toward the same common goals – alleviation of life's burdens and the expansion of discretionary time and spending power. Its role is profoundly different from what it has been for the ordinary corporation during its brief, turbulent, and remarkably protean history. It orchestrates the twin vectors of technology and globalization for the world's benefit. Neither fate, nor nature, nor God but rather the necessity of commerce created this role.

In the United States two industries became global long before they were consciously aware of it. After over a generation of persistent and acrimonious labor shutdowns, the United Steelworkers of America have not called an industrywide strike since 1959; the United Auto Workers have

not shut down General Motors since 1970. Both unions realize that they have become global – shutting down all or most of U.S. manufacturing would not shut out U.S. customers. Overseas suppliers are there to supply the market.

Cracking the code of Western markets

Since the theory of the marketing concept emerged a quarter of a century ago, the more managerially advanced corporations have been eager to offer what customers clearly wanted rather than what was merely convenient. They have created marketing departments supported by professional market researchers of awesome and often costly proportions. And they have proliferated extraordinary numbers of operations and product lines – highly tailored products and delivery systems for many different markets, market segments, and nations.

Significantly, Japanese companies operate almost entirely without marketing departments or market research of the kind so prevalent in the West. Yet, in the colorful words of General Electric's chairman John F. Welch, Jr., the Japanese, coming from a small cluster of resource-poor islands, with an entirely alien culture and an almost impenetrably complex language, have cracked the code of Western markets. They have done it not by looking with mechanistic thoroughness at the way markets are different but rather by searching for meaning with a deeper wisdom. They have discovered the one great thing all markets have in common—an overwhelming desire for dependable, world-standard modernity in all things, at aggressively low prices. In response, they deliver irresistible value everywhere, attracting people with products that market-research technocrats described with superficial certainty as being unsuitable and uncompetitive.

The wider a company's global reach, the greater the number of regional and national preferences it will encounter for certain product features, distribution systems, or promotional media. There will always need to be some accommodation to differences. But the widely prevailing and often unthinking belief in the immutability of these differences is generally mistaken. Evidence of business failure because of lack of accommodation is often evidence of other shortcomings.

Take the case of Revlon in Japan. The company unnecessarily alienated retailers and confused customers by selling world-standardized cosmetics only in elite outlets; then it tried to recover with low-priced world-standardized products in broader distribution, followed by a change in the company president and cutbacks in distribution as costs rose faster than sales. The problem was not that Revlon didn't understand the Japanese market; it didn't do the job right, wavered in its programs, and was impatient to boot.

By contrast, the Outboard Marine Corporation, with imagination, push, and persistence, collapsed long-established three-tiered distribution channels in Europe into a more focused and controllable two-step system—and did so despite the vociferous warnings of local trade groups. It also reduced the number and types of retail outlets. The result was greater improvement in credit and product-installation service to customers, major cost reductions, and sales advances.

In its highly successful introduction of Contac 600 (the timed-release decongestant) into Japan, SmithKline Corporation used 35 wholesalers instead of the 1,000-plus that established practice required. Daily contacts with the wholesalers and key retailers, also in violation of established practice, supplemented the plan, and it worked.

Denied access to established distribution institutions in the United States, Komatsu, the Japanese manufacturer of lightweight farm machinery, entered the market through over-the-road construction equipment dealers in rural areas of the Sunbelt, where farms are smaller, the soil sandier and easier to work. Here inexperienced distributors were able to attract customers on the basis of Komatsu's product and price appropriateness.

In cases of successful challenge to prevailing institutions and practices, a combination of product reliability and quality, strong and sustained support systems, aggressively low prices, and sales-compensation packages, as well as audacity and implacability, circumvented, shattered, and transformed very different distribution systems. Instead of resentment, there was admiration.

Still, some differences between nations are unyielding, even in a world of microprocessors. In the United States almost all manufacturers of microprocessors check them for reliability through a so-called parallel system of testing. Japan prefers the totally different sequential testing system. So Teradyne Corporation, the world's largest producer of microprocessor test equipment, makes one line for the United States and one for Japan. That's easy.

What's not so easy for Teradyne is to know how best to organize and manage, in this instance, its marketing effort. Companies can organize by product, region, function, or by using some combination of these. A company can have separate marketing organizations for Japan and for the United States, or it can have separate product groups, one working largely in Japan and the other in the United States. A single manufacturing facility or marketing operation might service both markets, or a company might use separate marketing operations for each.

Questions arise if the company organizes by product. In the case of Teradyne, should the group handling the parallel system, whose major market is the United States, sell in Japan and compete with the group focused on the Japanese market? If the company organizes regionally, how do regional groups divide their efforts between promoting the parallel vs. the sequential system? If the company organizes in terms of function, how does it get commitment in marketing, for example, for one line instead of the other?

There is no one reliably right answer—no one formula by which to get it. There isn't even a satisfactory contingent answer.[3] What works well for one company or one place may fail for another in precisely the same place, depending on the capabilities, histories, reputations, resources, and even the cultures of both.

The earth is flat

The differences that persist throughout the world despite its globalization affirm an ancient dictum of economics—that things are driven by what happens at the margin, not at the core. Thus, in ordinary competitive analysis, what's important is not the average price but the marginal price; what happens not in the usual case but at the interface of newly erupting conditions. What counts in commercial affairs is what happens at the cutting edge. What is most striking today is the underlying similarities of what is happening now to national preferences at the margin. These similarities at the cutting edge cumulatively form an overwhelming, predominant commonality everywhere.

To refer to the persistence of economic nationalism (protective and subsidized trade practices, special tax aids, or restrictions for home market producers) as a barrier to the globalization of markets is to make a valid point. Economic nationalism does have a powerful persistence. But, as with the present almost totally smooth internationalization of investment capital, the past alone does not shape or predict the future. (For reflections on the internationalization of capital, see the insert, "The shortening of Japanese horizons.")

Reality is not a fixed paradigm, dominated by immemorial customs and derived attitudes, heedless of powerful and abundant new forces. The world is becoming increasingly informed about the liberating and enhancing possibilities of modernity. The persistence of the inherited varieties of national preferences rests uneasily on increasing evidence of, and restlessness regarding, their inefficiency, costliness, and confinement. The historic past, and the national differences respecting commerce and industry it spawned and fostered everywhere, is now subject to relatively easy transformation.

Cosmopolitanism is no longer the monopoly of the intellectual and leisure classes; it is becoming the established property and defining characteristic of all sectors everywhere in the world. Gradually and irresistibly it breaks down the walls of economic insularity, nationalism, and chauvinism. What we see today as escalating commercial nationalism is simply the last violent death rattle of an obsolete institution.

Companies that adapt to and capitalize on economic convergence can still make distinctions and adjustments in different markets. Persistent differences in the world are consistent with fundamental underlying commonalities; they often complement rather than oppose each other—in business as they do in physics. There is, in physics, simultaneously matter and anti-matter working in symbiotic harmony.

The earth is round, but for most purposes it's sensible to treat it as flat. Space is curved, but not much for everyday life here on earth.

Divergence from established practice happens all the time. But the multinational mind,

The shortening of Japanese horizons

One of the most powerful yet least celebrated forces driving commerce toward global standardization is the monetary system, along with the international investment process.

Today money is simply electronic impulses. With the speed of light it moves effortlessly between distant centers (and even lesser places). A change of ten basis points in the price of a bond causes an instant and massive shift of money from London to Tokyo. The system has profound impact on the way companies operate throughout the world.

Take Japan, where high debt-to-equity balance sheets are "guaranteed" by various societal presumptions about the virtue of "a long view," or by government policy in other ways. Even here, upward shifts in interest rates in other parts of the world attract capital out of the country in powerful proportions. In recent years more and more Japanese global corporations have gone to the world's equity markets for funds. Debt is too remunerative in high-yielding countries to keep capital at home to feed the Japanese need. As interest rates rise, equity becomes a more attractive option for the issuer.

The long-term impact on Japanese enterprise will be transforming. As the equity proportion of Japanese corporate capitalization rises, companies will respond to the shorter-term investment horizons of the equity markets. Thus the much-vaunted Japanese corporate practice to taking the long view will gradually disappear.

warped into circumspection and timidity by years of stumbles and transnational troubles, now rarely challenges existing overseas practices. More often it considers any departure from inherited domestic routines as mindless, disrespectful, or impossible. It is the mind of a bygone day.

The successful global corporation does not abjure customization or differentiation for the requirements of markets that differ in product preferences, spending patterns, shopping preferences, and institutional or legal arrangements. But the global corporation accepts and adjusts to these differences only reluctantly, only after relentlessly testing their immutability, after trying in various ways to circumvent and reshape them as we saw in the cases of Outboard Marine in Europe, SmithKline in Japan, and Komatsu in the United States.

There is only one significant respect in which a company's activities around the world are important, and this is what it produces and how it sells. Everything else derives from, and is subsidiary to, these activities.

The purpose of business is to get and keep a customer. Or, to use Peter Drucker's more refined construction, to *create* and keep a customer. A

3 For a discussion of multinational reorganization, see Christopher A. Bartlett, "MNCs: Get Off the Reorganization Merry-Go-Round," HBR March-April 1983, p. 138.

company must be wedded to the ideal of innovation—offering better or more preferred products in such combinations of ways, means, places, and at such prices that prospects *prefer* doing business with the company rather than with others.

Preferences are constantly shaped and reshaped. Within our global commonality enormous variety constantly asserts itself and thrives, as can be seen within the world's single largest domestic market, the United States. But in the process of world homogenization, modern markets expand to reach cost-reducing global proportions. With better and cheaper communication and transport, even small local market segments hitherto protected from distant competitors now feel the pressure of their presence. Nobody is safe from global reach and the irresistible economies of scale.

Two vectors shape the world—technology and globalization. The first helps determine human preferences; the second, economic realities. Regardless of how much preferences evolve and diverge, they also gradually converge and form markets where economies of scale lead to reduction of costs and prices.

The modern global corporation contrasts powerfully with the aging multinational corporation. Instead of adapting to superficial and even entrenched differences within and between nations, it will seek sensibly to force suitably standardized products and practices on the entire globe. They are exactly what the world will take, if they come also with low prices, high quality, and blessed reliability. The global company will operate, in this regard, precisely as Henry Kissinger wrote in *Years of Upheaval* about the continuing Japanese economic success—"voracious in its collection of information, impervious to pressure, and implacable in execution."

Given what is everywhere the purpose of commerce, the global company will shape the vectors of technology and globalization into its great strategic fecundity. It will systematically push these vectors toward their own convergence, offering everyone simultaneously high-quality, more or less standardized products at optimally low prices, thereby achieving for itself vastly expanded markets and profits. Companies that do not adapt to the new global realities will become victims of those that do. ▽

Reprint 83308

The Pluralization of Consumption

The end of mass markets and mass marketing is constantly proclaimed. Evidence is suggested by the growing proliferation of products and brands in all categories, the miniaturization

of segments and sectors, and the multiplication of small market niches.

It would be a terrible mistake to believe this simple message, and disastrous to act upon it.

Things are not what they seem. The earth spins on its axis, rotates in an elliptical orbit, and regularly unleashes a bewildering and largely unpredictable variety of weathers and catastrophes. But it is not centrifugal, stationary, flat, or chaotic.

Markets are also not what they seem, though they seem suddenly proliferating and disorderly. A Copernican view suggests another interpretation to which no business can afford to be inattentive.

Every corner of the globe now gets increasingly subjected to the same intense and similar communications –commercial, cultural, social, and hard-news. Consequently, consciousness converges towards global commonality and modernity, cosmopolizing preferences and homogenizing consumption.

Yet, perversely, heterogeneity and parochialism thrive – religious dogmatism, raging nationalism, escalating ethnicity. And markets fragment, even within nations. Dozens of different detergent items congest the stores, automotive multiplicities clog the roads, and similar propagations accelerate in personal computers, engineering workstations, toiletries, TV transmission, convenience foods, cameras, financial services, health care, ready-to-eat cereals, apparel, soft drinks, machine tools, chemicals, airlines, magazines, polymers, jeans, retailing institutions, and on and on.

The more powerfully homogenizing and relentlessly globalized the world's communications and com-

merce get, the more varied its products and more numerous its consuming segments seem to become. The world suddenly looks remarkably Hegelian, even centrifugal.

But it would be wrong to characterize what we see as fragmentation or proliferation, or to view the obvious persistence of inherited local, national, and ethnic consuming preferences as contradicting the theory of global homogenization.

What changes does not disconfirm what endures. Absence of evidence is not evidence of absence. At some stage, established mass markets usually divide into lots of small specialty ones, except that now this happens sooner and faster, and that all the new segments show up everywhere.

The global boom in ethnic food specialties is a microcosm of what's happening in all product categories. Suddenly, in all the world's urban places the demand for ethnic fast foods thrives: pizza, hamburgers, sushi, frankfurters, Greek salad, Chinese egg rolls, pita bread, croissants, tapas, curry, bagels, chili, doughnuts, french fries, and even Sacher torte. Everybody who can get them wants them, regardless of national residence, origin, religion, tradition, or even taboos. Suddenly everybody everywhere simultaneously occupies each of these product-market segments – often several on a given day, even at a given eating occasion.

In all product categories and places, people increasingly occupy many and often disparate segments, and circulate among varied brands. Customer segments are no longer tightly discrete or distinct. Segments have become porous and coincident. Customers are now segment mi-

grants, possessed of multiple segment preferences at the same time. They've become heteroconsumers, as in a cafeteria, leading lives of seemingly idiosyncratic consumption.

Yet there's a converging rationality. Consider again the scrambled variety of ethnic food preferences. What people want is not just the variety of these foods, but their convenient, fast, low-cost, and nutritious availability. In that sense, everybody is in the same single segment, a segment that consists of people with plural preferences satisfiable in a similar convenient fashion.

We live suddenly in a world of segment simultaneity, the new world of the heteroconsumer. What's new is not the multiplication of segments but rather the pluralization of consumption.

It would be a bad mistake for a company to treat the plural consumer as if he or she were the occupant of a fixed and narrow segment. Most companies offer relatively wide lines of products, sizes, features, and forms in a given category. But mostly they do this for what have become the wrong reasons. The old right reasons were to have a line of items suitable specifically for each large, distinctive, and definable preference group. The new right reasons should be to have what serves and attracts people who've become increasingly alike and indistinct from one another, and yet have simultaneously varied and multiple preferences.

It would therefore also be a bad mistake to advertise a product or service as if the intended audience remained monolithic and singular, characterized demographically, psy-

dardization and pluralization – standardization in the sense that these preferences now appear everywhere, and pluralization in the sense that everywhere people want the same variety – in the stores, at home, in factories, fields, mines, offices, laboratories, schools, temples; regarding the sacred and the secular, work and play, study and diversion, reality and fantasy.

Nothing is exempt from the allure of new possibilities – for personal expression and fulfillment, for lightening work and enhancing life. Everybody is attracted to the multiple possibilities of modernity, including, coincidentally and paradoxically, the preservation of deeply remembered traditions and loyalties. They are deeply remembered and strongly coveted precisely because so much modernity is so alluring and unsettling. That helps explain the global eruptions of nationalistic, ethnic, and religious intensities. Humankind, said T.S. Eliot, cannot stand too much change or reality. It needs roots, remembrance, attachments, fantasy, and transcendence, while wanting simultaneously everything else that beckons within palpable reach.

Expanding are the possibilities of people having exactly what they

tively, similar small preferences in many places cumulate into global bigness in all places. No product category – consumer or industrial, tangible or intangible, consumable or durable – is exempt.

All products everywhere undergo the division of monolithic big segments into porous little ones. Though consumption thus gets pluralized and miniaturized, its global aggregate gets magnified. The competitive possibilities for scale and scope become compelling. Those who act on these possibilities capture economizing advantages that get envied and regretted by those who only sit and wait.

Few firms can escape the churn and necessities imposed by intensified global competition. Almost all companies will have to widen their geographic reach and offerings. Even those that choose to specialize geographically, or tightly in a narrow line, will have to operate globally. That is the only way to capture the scale economies necessary to get and keep costs down, get access to low-cost suppliers, and generate sufficient cash to finance the development and innovations that competitiveness requires.

Success therefore becomes a matter of combining global reach with

chologically, or functionally by a fixed structure of wants and wishes. This is no longer how things are, and it poses one of marketing's major creative challenges.

The challenge is global. The rapid acceleration of cheap and easy communication, transport, and travel globalizes competition and cosmopolizes consumption. The world's consumption preferences are driven simultaneously toward both stan-

wish as they wish things, and at mass-produced prices – prices that are low not so much because of improved or flexible manufacturing, but rather because of global scale economies. The kinds of small market segments common in Switzerland now also appear in Sri Lanka and Swaziland. Everywhere people learn from the same communal messenger, while prices descend into increasingly attractive reach. Addi-

local vigor, and of developing new, efficient ways to address and serve the heteroconsumer who is so ambidextrously engaged in pluralized consumption.

Ted Levitt

Reprint 88315

Customer Relations

After the sale is over…

'Relationship management' between buyers and sellers is much like that between husbands and wives

Theodore Levitt

As our economy becomes more service and technology oriented, the dynamics of the sales process will change. The ongoing nature of services and the growing complexity of technology will increasingly necessitate lengthy and involved relationships between buyers and sellers. Thus, the seller's focus will need to shift from simply landing sales to ensuring buyer satisfaction after the purchase. To keep buyers happy, vendors must maintain constructive interaction with purchasers – which includes keeping up on their complaints and future needs. Repeat orders will go to those sellers who have done the best job of nurturing these relationships, the author argues.

Of course, not all products and services require the same degree of relationship cultivating; the longer the period of time over which the service will be extended or the more complex the product being sold, the more attention the seller must give the relationship. Whatever effort is appropriate, though, must be made in a systematic and regular way, which means that sellers must be alert and sensitive. The author offers suggestions for incorporating these qualities into companies' business practices.

Mr. Levitt is the Edward W. Carter Professor of Business Administration and for the past seven years has been head of the marketing area at the Harvard Business School. With this article, he becomes HBR's most frequent contributor – 25 articles, beginning with "The Changing Character of Capitalism" (July-August 1956). His most recent articles are "The Globalization of Markets" (May-June 1983) and "Marketing Intangible Products and Product Intangibles" (May-June 1981). His seventh book, The Marketing Imagination, was published in Fall 1983 by Free Press.

The relationship between a seller and a buyer seldom ends when a sale is made. Increasingly, the relationship intensifies after the sale and helps determine the buyer's choice the next time around. Such dynamics are found particularly with services and products dealt in a stream of transactions between seller and buyer – financial services, consulting, general contracting, military and space equipment, and capital goods.

The sale, then, merely consummates the courtship, at which point the marriage begins. How good the marriage is depends on how well the seller manages the relationship. The quality of the marriage determines whether there will be continued or expanded business, or troubles and divorce. In some cases divorce is impossible, as when a major construction or installation project is underway. If the marriage that remains is burdened, it tarnishes the seller's reputation.

Companies can avoid such troubles by recognizing at the outset the necessity of managing their relationships with customers. This takes special attention to an often ignored aspect of relationships: time.

The theory of supply and demand presumes that the work of the economic system is time-discrete and bare of human interaction – that an instantaneous, disembodied sales transaction clears the market at the intersection of supply and demand.

Author's note:
This article profited immensely from work done by James L. Crimmins, president of Business Times, Inc., the morning business news show on ESPN Cable, and his colleagues at Playback Associates.

This was never completely accurate and has become less so as product complexity and interdependencies have intensified. Buyers of automated machinery do not, like buyers at a flea market, walk home with their purchases and take their chances. They expect installation services, application aids, parts, postpurchase repair and maintenance, retrofitted enhancements, and vendor R&D to keep the products effective and up to date for as long as possible and to help the company stay competitive.

The buyer of a continuous stream of transactions, like a frozen-food manufacturer that buys its cartons from a packaging company and its cash-management services from a bank, is concerned not only with completing transactions but also with maintaining the process. Due to the growing complexity of military equipment, even the Department of Defense makes most of its purchases in units of less than a hundred and therefore has to repeat transactions often.

Because the purchase cycles of products and major components are increasingly stretched, the needs that must be tended to have changed. Consider the purchase cycles and the changing assurances backing purchases (see *Exhibit I*). Under these conditions, a purchase decision is not a decision to buy an item (to have a casual affair) but a decision to enter a bonded relationship (to get married). This requires of the would-be seller a new orientation and a new strategy.

Selling by itself is no longer enough. Consider the compelling differences between the old and the new selling arrangements *Exhibit II* illustrates. In the selling scheme the seller is located at a distance from buyers and reaches out with a sales department to unload products on them. This is the basis for the notion that a salesperson needs charisma, because it is charisma rather than the product's qualities that makes the sale.

Consider, by contrast, marketing. Here the seller, being physically close to buyers, penetrates their domain to learn about their needs, desires, and fears and then designs and supplies the product with those considerations in mind. Instead of trying to get buyers to want what the seller has, the seller tries to have what they want. The "product" is no longer merely an item but a whole bundle of values that satisfy buyers—an "augmented" product.[1]

Thanks to increasing interdependence, more and more of the world's economic work gets done through long-term relationships between sellers and buyers. It is not a matter of just getting and then holding on to customers. It is more a matter of giving the buyers what they want. Buyers want vendors who keep promises, who'll keep supplying and standing

---

1 See my article "Marketing Success Through Differentiation—Of Anything," HBR January-February 1980, p. 83.

Exhibit I Purchase cycles and assurances

Item	Purchase cycle in years	
Oil field installation	15 to 20	
Chemical plant	10 to 15	
EDP system	5 to 10	
Weapons system	20 to 30	
Major components of steel plant	5 to 10	
Paper supply contract	5	

Item	Previous assurance	Present assurance
Tankers	Spot	Charter
Apartments	Rental	Cooperative
Auto warranties	10,000 miles	100,000 miles
Technology	Buy	Lease
Labor	Hire	Contracts
Supplies	Shopping	Contracting
Equipment	Repair	Maintenance

Exhibit II The change from selling to marketing

Selling

Marketing

behind what they promised. The era of the one-night stand is gone. Marriage is both necessary and more convenient. Products are too complicated, repeat negotiations too much of a hassle and too costly. Under these conditions, success in marketing is transformed into the inescapability of a relationship. Interface becomes interdependence.

Under these circumstances, being a good marketer in the conventional sense is not enough. When it takes five years of intensive work between seller and buyer to "deliver" an operating chemical plant or a telecommunications system, much more is required than the kind of marketing that simply lands the contract. The buyer needs assurance at the outset that the two parties can work well together during the long period in which the purchase gets transformed into delivery.

The seller and the buyer have different capital structures, competitive conditions, costs, and incentives driving the commitments they make to each other. The seller has made a sale that is expected to yield a profit. The buyer has bought a tool with which to produce things to yield a profit. For the seller it is the end of the process; for the buyer, only the beginning. Yet their interdependence is inescapable and profound. To make these differently motivated dependencies work, the selling company must understand the relationship and plan its management in advance of the wedding. It can't get out the marriage manual only after trouble has begun.

The product's changing nature

The future will be marked by intense business relationships in all areas of marketing, including frequently purchased consumer goods. Procter & Gamble, copying General Mills's Betty Crocker advisory service, has found that the installation of a consumer hot line to give advice on its products and their uses has cemented customer brand loyalty.

In the industrial setting we have only to review changing perceptions of various aspects of product characteristics to appreciate the new emphasis on relationships (see *Exhibit III*). The common characteristic of the terms in the "future" column of this exhibit is time. What is labeled "item" in the first column was in the past simply a product, something that was bought for its own value. More recently that simple product has not been enough. Instead, buyers have bought augmented products.

During the era we are entering the emphasis will be on systems contracts, and buyer-seller relationships will be characterized by continuous contact and evolving relationships to effect the systems. The "sale" will be not just a system but a system over time. The value at stake will be the advantages of that total system over time. As the customer gains experience, the technology will decline in importance relative to the system that enables the buyer to realize the benefits of the technology. Services, delivery, reliability, responsiveness, and the quality of the human and organizational interactions between seller and buyer will be more important than the technology itself.

The more complex the system and the more "software" (including operating procedures and protocols, management routines, service components) it requires, the greater the customer's anxieties and expectations. People buy expectations, not things. They buy the expectations of benefits promised by the vendor. When it takes a long time to fulfill the promise (to deliver a new custom-made automated work station, for example) or when fulfillment is continual over a long period (as it is in banking services, fuel deliveries, or shipments of components for assembly operations), the buyer's anxieties build up after the purchase decision is made. Will the delivery be prompt? Will it be smooth and regular? Did we select the best vendor?

Differing expectations

When downstream realities loom larger than up-front promises, what do you do before, during, and after the sale? Who should be responsible for what?

To answer these questions it helps to understand how the promises and behavior of the vendor before the sale is made shape the customer's expectations. It is reasonable for a customer who has been promised the moon to expect it to be delivered. But if those who make the promises are paid commissions before the customer gets everything he bargained for, they're not likely to feel compelled to ensure that the customer gets fully satisfied later. After the sale, they'll rush off to pursue other prey. If marketing plans the sale, sales makes it, manufacturing fulfills it, and service services it, who's in charge and who takes responsibility for the whole process?

Problems arise not only because those who do the selling, the marketing, the manufacturing, and the servicing have varying incentives and views of the customer but also because organizations are one-dimensional. People, with the exception of those who work in sales or marketing, seldom see beyond their company's walls. For those inside those walls, inside is where the work gets done, where the penalties and incentives are doled out, where the budgets and plans

Exhibit III	Perceptions of product values		
Category	Past	Present	Future
Item	Product	Augmented product	System contracts
Sale	Unit	System	System over time
Value	Feature advantages	Technology advantages	System advantages
Leadtime	Short	Long	Lengthy
Service	Modest	Important	Vital
Delivery place	Local	National	Global
Delivery phase	Once	Often	Continually
Strategy	Sales	Marketing	Relationship

Exhibit IV	Varying reactions and perceptions before and during sale process

When the sale is first made

Seller	Buyer
Objective achieved.	Judgment postponed; applies test of time.
Selling stops.	Shopping continues.
Focus goes elsewhere.	Focus on purchase; wants affirmation that expectations have been met.
Tension released.	Tension increased.
Relationship reduced or ended.	Commitment made; relationship intensified.

Throughout the process

Stage of sale		Seller	Buyer
1	Before	Real hope	Vague need
2	Romance	Hot & heavy	Testing & hopeful
3	Sale	Fantasy: bed	Fantasy: board
4	After	Looks elsewhere for next sale	"You don't care"
5	Long after	Indifferent	"Can't this be made better?"
6	Next sale	"How about a new one?"	"Really?"

get made, where engineering and manufacturing are done, where performance is measured, where one's friends and associates gather, where things are managed and manageable. Outside "has nothing to do with me" and is where "you can't change things."

Many disjunctions exist between seller and buyer at various stages of the sales process. These may be simply illustrated, as in *Exhibit IV.*

After the fact

The fact of buying changes the dynamics of the relationship. The buyer expects the seller to remember the purchase as having been a favor bestowed, not as something earned by the seller. Hence it is wrong to assume that getting an account gives you an advantage because you've got a foot in the door. The opposite is more often the case. The buyer that views the sale as a favor conferred on the seller in effect debits the seller's account. The seller owes the buyer one. He is in the position of having to rebuild the relationship from a deficit stance.

In the absence of good management, the relationship deteriorates because both organizations tend naturally to face inward rather than outward toward each other. The natural tendency of relationships, whether in marriage or in business, is toward erosion of sensitivity and attentiveness. Inward orientation by the selling organization leads to insensitivity and unresponsiveness in customer relations. At best the company substitutes bureaucratic formalities for authentic interaction.

A healthy relationship maintains, and preferably expands, the equity and the possibilities that were created during courtship. A healthy relationship requires a conscious and constant fight against the forces of decline. It becomes important for the seller regularly and seriously to consider whether the relationship is improving or deteriorating, whether the promises are being completely fulfilled, whether he is neglecting anything, and how he stands vis-à-vis his competitors. *Exhibit V* compares actions that affect— for better or worse—relationships with buyers.

Building dependencies

One of the surest signs of a bad or declining relationship is the absence of complaints from the customer. Nobody is ever *that* satisfied, especially not over an extended period of time. The customer is either not being candid or not being contacted.

Probably both. The absence of candor reflects the decline of trust and the deterioration of the relationship. Bad things accumulate. Impaired communication is both a symptom and a cause of trouble. Things fester inside. When they finally erupt, it's usually too late or too costly to correct the situation.

We can invest in relationships and we can borrow from them. We all do both, but we seldom account for our actions and almost never manage them. Yet a company's most precious asset is its relationships with its customers. What matters is not whom you know but how you are known to them.

Not all relationships can or need be of the same duration or at the same level of intimacy. These factors depend on the extent of the actual or felt dependency between the buyer and the seller. And of course those dependencies can be extended or contracted through various direct links that can be established between the two parties. Thus, when Bergen Brunswig, the booming drug and health care products distributor, puts computer terminals in its customers' offices to enable them to order directly and get instant feedback regarding their sales and inventory, it creates a new link that helps tie the customer to the vendor.

At the same time, however, the seller can become dependent on the buyer in important ways. Most obvious is vendor reliance on the buyer for a certain percentage of its sales. More subtle is reliance on the buyer for important information, including how the buyer's business will change, how changes will affect future purchases, and what competitors are offering in the way of substitute products or materials, at what prices and including which services. The buyer can also answer questions like these for the vendor: How well is the vendor fulfilling the customer's needs? Is performance up to promises from headquarters? To what new uses is the customer putting the product?

The seller's ability to forecast the buyer's intentions rests on the quality of the overall relationship. In a good relationship the buyer shares plans and expectations with the vendor, or at least makes available relevant information. With that information the vendor can better serve the buyer. Surprises and bad forecasts are symptoms of bad relationships. In such instances, everybody—even the buyer—loses.

Thus, a system of reciprocal dependencies develops. It is up to the seller to nurture the relationship beyond its simple dollar value. In a proper relationship both the buyer and the seller will benefit or the relationship will not last.

Moreover, both parties should understand that the seller's expenses rarely end with acquisition costs. This means that the vendor should work at convincing the customer of the importance of maintaining the vendor's long-term profitability at a comfortable level instead of squeezing to get rock-bottom delivered prices. Unless the costs of the expected post-

Exhibit V	Actions that affect relationships	
	Positive actions	**Negative actions**
	Initiate positive phone calls	Make only call backs
	Make recommendations	Make justifications
	Use candid language	Use accommodative language
	Use phone	Use correspondence
	Show appreciation	Wait for misunderstandings
	Make service suggestions	Wait for service requests
	Use "we" problem-solving language	Use "owe us" legal language
	Get to problems	Respond only to problems
	Use jargon or shorthand	Use long-winded communications
	Air personality problems	Hide personality problems
	Talk of "our future together"	Talk about making good on the past
	Routinize responses	Fire drill/emergency responsiveness
	Accept responsibility	Shift blame
	Plan the future	Rehash the past

Exhibit VI Cumulative cash flow history of an account

purchase services are reflected in the price, the buyer will end up paying extra in money, in delays, and in aggravation. The smart relationship manager in the selling company will help the buyer do long-term life-cycle costing to assess the vendor's offering.

Bonds that last

Professional partnerships in law, medicine, architecture, consulting, investment banking, and advertising rate and reward associates by their client relationships. Like any other assets, these relationships can appreciate or depreciate. Their maintenance and enhancement depend not so much on good manners, public relations, tact, charm, window dressing, or manipulation as they do on management. Relationship management requires companywide maintenance, investment, improvement, and even replacement programs. The results can be spectacular.

Examine the case of the North Sea oil and gas fields. Norway and Britain urged and facilitated exploration and development of those resources. They were eager and even generous hosts to the oil companies. The companies, though they spent hundreds of millions of dollars to do the work, didn't fully nurture their relationships. When oil and gas suddenly started to flow, the host countries levied taxes exceeding 90% of the market prices. No one was more surprised than the companies. Why should they have been surprised? Had they built sound relationships with the governments, the politicians, and the voters—by whatever means—so as to have created a sense of mutuality and partnership, they might have moderated the size of the taxes. What would it have been worth?

This is not an isolated occurrence. The same problem crops up in similar circumstances where vendors are required to make heavy expenditures to get accounts and develop products. *Exhibit VI* depicts cash flows to a vendor of this type during the life of the account. During the customer-getting and development period, cash flows are negative and the customer eagerly encourages the expenditures. When the product is delivered or the joint venture becomes operative, cumulative cash flows turn up and finally become positive. In the case of the North Sea, the surprising new high taxes represent the difference between what revenues to the oil companies might have been (the upper level of potential revenue) and what they actually became. With worse relationships they might, of course, have fallen to an even lower level of potential revenue.

Consider also the case of Gillette North America. It has four separate sales forces and special programs for major accounts to ensure Gillette's rapid and smooth response to customers' requirements. Gillette also has a vice president of business relations who has among his major duties cultivation of relationships with major retailers and distributors. He carries out that responsibility via a vast array of ceremonial activities ranging from entertainment at trade association conventions to organization of special events for major accounts in connection with the annual All-Star baseball game, the World Series, the Superbowl, and the NCAA playoffs. These activities establish bonds and affirm reciprocal obligations and benefits.

Some companies now require engineering and manufacturing people to spend time with customers and users in the field—not just to get product and design ideas or feedback regarding present products but also to get to know and to respond to customers in deep and abiding ways so as to build relationships and bonds that last. The Sperry Corporation's much-advertised "listening" campaign has included training employees to listen and communicate effectively with each other and with customers.

All too often company officials take action instead of spending time. It is all too easy to act first and later try to fix the relationship, instead of the other way around. It is all too simple to say, "We'll look into it and call you back" or "Let's get together for lunch sometime." These are tactics of diversion and delay, not of relationship building.

When a purchase cycle is long—as when a beer-making plant contracts with a can-making vendor to build a factory next door or when the U.S. Air Force commits itself to buying a jet engine with a life of 20 to 30 years—the people in the vendor organization who did the selling and those in the customer organization who did the buying will be replaced over the course of those relationships. So, in all likelihood, will the entire upper levels of management on both sides. What must the seller do to ensure continuity of good relations? What is expected of the customer when people who did the buying are changed and gone? Clearly the idea is to build bonds that last no matter who comes and goes.

Making it happen

To effectively manage relationships, managers must meet four requirements:

1   **Awareness.** Understand both the problem and the opportunity areas.

2   **Assessment.** Determine where the company now stands, especially in terms of what's necessary to get the desired results.

3   **Accountability.** Establish regular reporting on individual relationships, and then on group relationships, so that these can be weighed against other measures of performance.

4   **Actions.** Make decisions and allocations and establish routines and communications on the basis of their impact on the targeted relationships. Constantly reinforce awareness and actions.

Relationship management can be institutionalized, but in the process it must also be humanized. One company has regular sensitivity sessions and role-playing seminars in which sales officials assume the buyer role. It also conducts debriefings on meetings with customers. And it requires its customer-contact people (including those who make deliveries and handle receivables) to regularly ask of various accounts the seminal questions: How are we doing in the relationship? Is it going up or down? Are we talking with the right people about the right issues? What have we *not* done lately?

The emphasis on "lately" is not incidental. It reflects the recognition that relationships naturally degrade and have to be reinvigorated. If I owe you a favor, I forget – but you don't. And when I've done you a favor, you feel obligated – but not for long. You ask, "What have you done for me lately?" A relationship credit must be cashed in or it expires, and it must be used soon or it depreciates.

Another way companies can institutionalize relationship management is by establishing routines that ensure the right kinds of customer contacts. A well-known Wall Street investment firm requires its security analysts and salespeople to make regular "constructive" contacts with their institutional customers. *Constructive* is defined as conveying useful information to them. The firm has set up a regular Monday-morning investment strategy "commentary" that analysts and salespeople can convey by telephone to their customers. In addition, each analyst must develop periodic industry commentaries and updates, to be mailed or telephoned to customers. Analysts and salespeople are required to keep logs of these contacts, which are compiled, counted, and communicated to all in a weekly companywide report. Those salespeople and analysts making the fewest contacts have to explain their inaction to supervisors.

The firm allocates end-of-year bonuses on the basis of not only commissions earned from the various institutions but also the number and types of contacts initiated and maintained. Meanwhile, the firm conducts regular sensitivity-training sessions to enhance the contacts and the quality of the relationships. The results, which show that the efforts have been highly successful, are analyzed and made known to all, thus reinforcing the importance of the process.

Relationship management is a special field all its own and is as important to preserving and enhancing the intangible asset commonly known as "goodwill" as is the management of hard assets. The fact that it is probably more difficult makes hard work at it that much more important. ▽

Reprint 83511

Product Differentiation

Marketing success through differentiation— of anything

Any product or service can be differentiated, even the commodity that seems to differ from competitors' offerings only in price

Theodore Levitt

On television we see product differentiation all the time, whether the subject of the commercial is a distinguishable good like an automobile or an indistinguishable good like laundry detergent. These are packaged products. How does the marketer differentiate a so-called commodity like isopropyl alcohol, strip steel, commercial bank services, or even legal counsel? The author describes the attributes of products that give the marketer opportunity to win the customer from the competition and, having won him, to keep him. Finally, the author describes the alert, imaginative state of mind that characterizes good management of product differentiation. "The way in which the manager operates becomes an extension of product differentiation," he says.

Mr. Levitt is the Edward W. Carter Professor of Business Administration at the Harvard Business School and head of the marketing area of instruction there. His articles in HBR, which number nearly two dozen, include the well-known "Marketing Myopia" (published in 1960 and reprinted as an HBR Classic in September-October 1975) and "Marketing When Things Change" (November-December 1977). His most recent book is *Marketing for Business Growth* (McGraw-Hill, 1974).

There is no such thing as a commodity. All goods and services are differentiable. Though the usual presumption is that this is more true of consumer goods than of industrial goods and services, the opposite is the actual case.

In the marketplace, differentiation is everywhere. Everybody—producer, fabricator, seller, broker, agent, merchant—tries constantly to distinguish his offering from all others. This is true even of those who produce and deal in primary metals, grains, chemicals, plastics, and money.

Fabricators of consumer and industrial goods seek competitive distinction via product features—some visually or measurably identifiable, some cosmetically implied, and some rhetorically claimed by reference to real or suggested hidden attributes that promise results or values different from those of competitors' products.

So too with consumer and industrial services—what I call, to be accurate, "intangibles." On the commodities exchanges, for example, dealers in metals, grains, and pork bellies trade in totally undifferentiated generic products. But what they "sell" is the claimed distinction of their execution—the efficiency of their transactions in thir clients' behalf, their responsiveness to inquiries, the clarity and speed of their confirmations, and the like. In short, the *offered* product is differentiated, though the *generic* product is identical.

When the generic product is undifferentiated, the offered product makes the difference in getting customers and the delivered product in keeping them. When the knowledgeable senior partner of a well-known Chicago brokerage firm appeared at a New York City bank in a tight-fitting, lime green polyester suit and Gucci shoes to solicit business in financial instrument futures, the outcome was predictably poor. The unintended offering implied by his sartorial appearance contradicted the intended offering of his carefully prepared presentation. No wonder that Thomas Watson the elder insisted so uncompromisingly that his salesmen be attired in their famous IBM "uniforms." While clothes may not make the man, they may help make the sale.

The usual presumption about so-called undifferentiated commodities is that they are exceedingly price sensitive. A fractionally lower price gets the business. That is seldom true except in the imagined world of economics textbooks. In the actual world of markets, nothing is exempt from other considerations, even when price competition rages.

During periods of sustained surplus, excess capacity, and unrelieved price war, when the attention of all seems riveted on nothing save price, it is precisely because price is visible and measurable, and potentially devastating in its effects, that price deflects attention from the possibilities of extricating the product from ravaging price competition. These possibilities, even in the short run, are not confined simply to nonprice competition, such as harder personal selling, intensified advertising, or what's loosely called more or better "services."

To see fully what these possibilities are, it is useful first to examine what exactly a product is.

What's a product?

Products are almost always combinations of the tangible and the intangible. An automobile is not simply a machine for movement visibly or measurably differentiated by design, size, color, options, horsepower, or miles per gallon. It is also a complex symbol denoting status, taste, rank, achievement, aspiration, and (these days) being "smart"—that is, buying fuel economy rather than display. But the customer buys even more than these attributes. The enormous efforts of the auto manufacturers to cut the time between placement and delivery of an order and to select, train, supervise, and motivate their dealerships suggest that these too are integral parts of the products people buy and are therefore ways by which products may be differentiated.

In the same way, a computer is not simply a machine for data storage and processing; it is also an operating system with special software protocols for use and promises of maintenance and repair. Carbon fibers are chemical additives that enhance flexuous stiffness, reduce weight, fight fatigue and corrosion, and cut fabrication costs when combined with certain other materials. But carbon fibers have no value for an inexperienced user without the design and applications help that only the experienced seller can provide.

In thousand-page contract proposals by government contractors or five-page consulting proposals to industrial clients, the product is a promise whose commercial substance resides as much in the proposer's carefully curried reputation (or "image") and in the proposal's meticulous packaging as it does in its physical content.

When the substantive content of the products of competing vendors are scarcely differentiable, sales power shifts to differentiating distinctions by which buyers may be influenced. In this regard, there is scant substantive difference among all that's done by Morgan Stanley & Co., Lockheed, McKinsey & Co., and Revlon. Though each will vigorously proclaim commanding generic distinctions vis-à-vis competitors, each is profoundly preoccupied with packaging—that is, with representing itself as unique. And, indeed, each may be unique, but its uniqueness resides most powerfully in things that transcend its generic offerings.

Take investment banking. Underwriters promise money to issuers and suggest similar promises to buyers. But how these promises are packaged profoundly influences both issuers and buyers. Consider this quotation from a close observer of the industry: "One eminent [U.S. investment banking] house has entrances on two streets, with different stationery printed for each entrance. One door is intended to be more exclusive than the other, and a visitor supposedly can tell the firm's assessment of his importance by the entrance indicated on the letterhead of the stationery he receives." [1] Obviously, the distinctions being made are selling devices based on the assumption that VIP treatment of certain visitors at reception will persuade them of VIP results later in actuality.

To the potential buyer, a product is a complex cluster of value satisfactions. The generic thing is not itself the product; it is merely, as in poker, table stakes—the minimum that is necessary at the outset to give its producer a chance to play the game. It is the playing that gets the results, and in business this means getting and keeping customers.

A customer attaches value to a product in proportion to its perceived ability to help solve his problems or meet his needs. All else is derivative. As a specialist in industrial marketing has expressed it,

"The 'product'... is the total package of benefits the customer receives when he buys."[2]

Consider the pragmatism of the Detroit auto manufacturers in buying sheet steel. Detroit buys to exceedingly tight technical specifications, but it specifies much more than the steel itself. It also demands certain delivery conditions and flexibilities, price and payment conditions, and reordering responsiveness. From year to year, the Detroit companies shift the proportions of steel they buy from their various suppliers on the basis of elaborate grading systems that measure each supplier's performance on the specified conditions, including the kind and quality of unsolicited help on such matters as new materials ideas, ideas for parts redesign, and even purchasing procedures.

Clearly, Detroit buys a bundle of value satisfactions of which the generic product is only a small portion. If, say, the delivery conditions and flexibilities are not fulfilled—or if they are fulfilled erratically, grudgingly, or only partially—the customer is not getting the product he expects. If, moreover, one supplier is more effectively active with new facilitating ideas, his "product" is better than his competitors'. Detroit sees with supreme clarity that No. 302, 72-inch, hot-rolled strip carbon steel is not a commodity. It is a measurably differentiated product.

The customer never just buys the "generic" product like steel, or wheat, or subassemblies, or investment banking, or aspirin, or engineering consultancy, or golf balls, or industrial maintenance, or newsprint, or cosmetics, or even 99% pure isopropyl alcohol. He buys something that transcends these designations—and what that "something" is helps determine from whom he'll buy, what he'll pay, and whether, in the view of the seller, he's "loyal" or "fickle."

What that something is in its customer-getting and customer-satisfying entirety can be managed. To see how it can be managed, it is helpful to look at the process graphically. *Exhibit I* (next page) does this by suggesting that a product consists of a range of possibilities, which I shall now describe.

The generic product

The fundamental, but rudimentary, substantive "thing" that's the table stakes of business—what's needed for a chance to play the game of market participation—is the *generic product*. It is, for the steel producer, the steel itself—or, in the Detroit example, No. 302, 72-inch, hot-rolled strip, or some-body's technical equivalent. For a bank, it's loanable funds. For a realtor, it's for-sale properties. For a retailer, it's a store with a certain mix of vendables. For a lawyer, it's having passed the bar exam.

Not all generic products are the same. Having passed the New York bar exam is not the same as having passed the Colorado exam. Because of slight differences among automobile company manufacturing processes, one supplier's "302" may, in fact, be "better" than another's. One mill's 302 may take certain coatings more easily or quickly than another's. One supplier may fill orders from a single mill, and another from several. In the latter case, the sheen or hue of the generic product may vary slightly from mill to mill, which makes considerable difference in the case of stainless steel that is used for decorative trim.

In most cases, these differences are not salient. More important are the characteristics of the expected components of the product.

The expected product

In *Exhibit I* the *expected product* is everything within the outer and inner gray circles, including the generic product. It represents the customer's minimal purchase conditions. What, for example, does the customer consider absolutely essential in strip steel?

1. *Delivery:* At what plants? When? Not just on what day, but at what hours of each day, so as to minimize valuable space for backup stock and to reduce inventory costs? The supplier has to be "logistically even" with the buyer. The proper quantity and flexibility—that is, quick and hassle-free responsiveness to snags in delivery quantities and times—are also expected. Finally, preferential treatment may be specified in case of shortages.

2. *Terms:* Specific prices for specific quantities for specific lengths of time. In the case of a change in list prices, the terms contain negotiable parameters, perhaps linked to such indexes as moving price averages of scrap and other steel-making ingredients over specified periods. The terms may also be reflected in discount structures related to the promptness of payment and add-on provisions for extended payment periods.

1. Samuel L. Hayes, III, "Investment Banking: Power Structure in Flux," HBR March-April 1971, p. 136.

2. E. Raymond Corey, "Key Options in Market Selection and Product Planning," HBR September-October 1975, p. 119. For an elaboration, see his *Industrial Marketing: Cases and Concepts* (Englewood Cliffs, N.J.: Prentice-Hall, 1976), pp. 40-41; also, see Benson P. Shapiro, "Making Money Through Marketing," HBR July-August 1979, p. 136.

Exhibit I
The total product concept

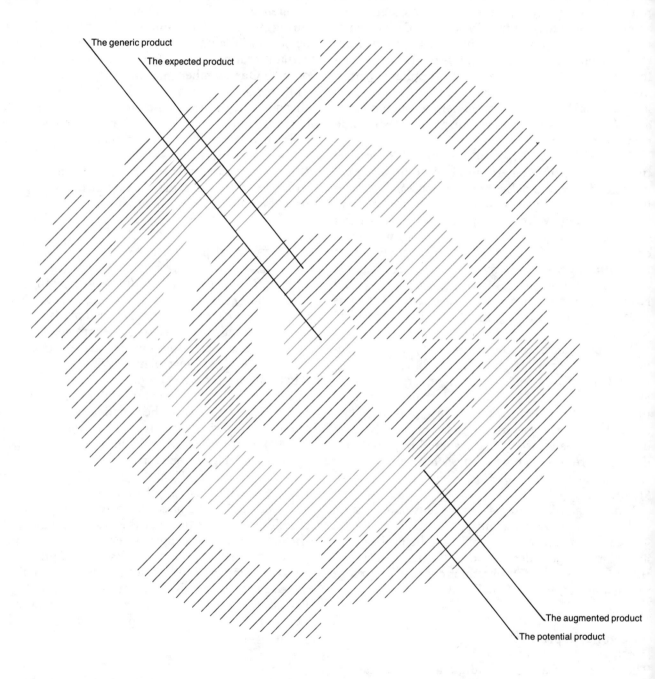

The generic product

The expected product

The augmented product

The potential product

3. *Support efforts:* Depending on what the uses of the product are, the purchaser may expect special applications advice and support.

4. *New ideas:* A normal expectation may include suppliers' ideas and suggestions for more efficient and cost-reducing ways of using the generic product in its various intended forms, such as fabrication, coating, and fastening.

All this may be well known, but the underlying principles encompass much more. The failure to fulfill certain more subtle expectations may reflect unfavorably on the generic product. A shabby brokerage office may cost a realtor access to customers for his for-sale properties. Even though the lawyer performed brilliantly in the bar exam and occupies offices of prudential elegance, his personality may clash with a potential client's. A manufacturer's competitively priced machine tools might have the most sophisticated of numerical controls tucked tightly behind an impressive panel, but certain customers may refuse to buy because output tolerances are more precise than necessary or usable. The customer may actually expect and want less.

The generic product can be sold only if the customer's wider expectations are met. Different means may be employed to meet those expectations. Hence differentiation follows expectation.

The augmented product

Differentiation is not limited to giving the customer what he expects. What he expects may be augmented by things he has never thought about. When a computer manufacturer implants a diagnostic module that automatically locates the source of failure or breakdown inside his equipment (as some now do), he has taken the product beyond what was required or expected by the buyer. It has become an *augmented product.* When a securities brokerage firm includes with its customers' monthly statements a current balance sheet for each customer and an analysis of sources and disposition of funds, that firm has augmented its product beyond what was required or expected by the buyer. When a manufacturer of health and beauty aids offers warehouse management advice and training programs for the employees of its distributors, that company too has augmented its product beyond what was required or expected by the buyer.

These voluntary or unprompted "augmentations" to the expected product are shown in *Exhibit I* by the irregular band that surrounds the expected product.

In every case, the supplier has exceeded the normal expectations of the buyer. In the case of our steel example, it can be done by developing better ways of fabricating and coating the product or by reducing thickness to cut weight. The seller may provide other unexpected but moderately helpful aids, such as new delivery scheduling ideas, more "interesting" terms, different ways of delivering batches so as to reduce the buyer's handling problems and costs, and invoicing systems that give the buyer more information about the use patterns of the generic product by his various plants, divisions, or brands.

Not all customers for all products and under all circumstances, however, can be attracted by an ever-expanding bundle of differentiating value satisfactions. Some customers may prefer lower prices to product augmentation. Some cannot use the extra services offered. Steel users, for instance, once dependent on mills for applications help and engineering support, gradually grew sufficiently sophisticated to free themselves of that dependence—a freedom which, incidentally, led to the rapid growth of independent steel distribution centers in competition with the mills.

(Now the centers, which have distinguished themselves from the mills by faster delivery on standard grades and sizes, a wider item mix, and ability to handle small orders, have augmented *their* product by doing more minor fabricating and adding certain specialty steel application services.)

As a rule, the more a seller expands the market by teaching and helping customers to use his product, the more vulnerable he becomes to losing them. When a customer no longer needs help, he gains the flexibility to shop for things he values more—such as price.

At this point, it makes sense to embark on a systematic program of customer-benefiting, and therefore customer-keeping, product augmentation. The seller should also, of course, focus on cost and price reduction. And that's the irony of product maturity: precisely when price competition heightens, and therefore when cost reduction becomes more important, is when the seller is also likely to benefit by incurring the additional costs of new product augmentation.

The augmented product is a condition of a mature market or of relatively experienced or sophisticated customers. Not that they could not benefit from or would not respond to extra services; but when a customer knows or thinks he knows everything and can do anything, the seller must test that assumption lest he be condemned to the purgatory of price competition alone. The best way to test the customer's assumption that he no longer needs or wants all or any part of the augmented product is to consider what's possible to offer that customer.

The potential product

Everything that might be done to attract and hold customers is what can be called the *potential product*. For the steel user, the offering may include:

> Suggested technical changes, such as redesign of a component to reduce weight, add strength or durability, cut lateral flex, improve adhesion and desirability of coatings, or enhance safety.

> Market research findings regarding customers' attitudes toward, and their problems with, the various alternatives to steel (plastics and aluminum, for example).

> New methods and technologies for shaping, forming, and fastening steel to steel, steel to plastics, and the like.

> New ideas for lubricants, noise-reducing materials, buffers, and gaskets.

> Tested proposals for easier, faster, and cheaper assembly systems.

> New ideas for varying product characteristics for various user segments, such as commercial fleets, taxi fleets, and rental companies, each of which has its own buying criteria.

> Concrete, tested suggestions for combining materials like steel and fiberglass.

Only the budget and the imagination limit the possibilities. But what the budget is and ought to be is often a function of what is necessary to being competitive in all the dimensions of the potential product.

Things will vary with conditions—economic conditions and competitive conditions. Competition may be a function not simply of what other steel suppliers offer but also of what suppliers of substitute materials offer. Reordering responsiveness is not nearly as important to buyers in good times as in bad—except when a competitor strategically uses the good times (that is, when demand is high and supply short) to accommodate a large prospective customer in order to get a foot in the door.

Economic conditions, business strategies, customers' wishes, competitive conditions, and much more can determine what sensibly defines the product. Nor are the ingredients of the described classifications fixed. What's "augmented" for one customer may be "expected" by another; what's "augmented" under one circumstance may be "potential" in another; part of what's "generic" in periods of short supply may be "expected" in periods of oversupply.

As with most things in business, nothing is simple, static, or explained very reliably by textbook taxonomies. One thing is certain: there is no such thing as a commodity—or, at least, from a competitive point of view, there need not be. Everything is differentiable, and, in fact, usually is differentiated. (See the ruled insert on next page.)

Role of management

The way a company manages its marketing can become the most powerful form of differentiation. Indeed, that may be how some companies in the same industry differ most from one another.

Brand management and product management are marketing tools that have demonstrable advantages over catchall, functional modes of management. The same is true of market management, a system widely employed when a particular tangible or intangible product is used in many different industries. Putting somebody in charge of a product that's used the same way by a large segment of the market (as in the case of packaged detergents sold through retail channels) or putting somebody in charge of a market for a product that's used differently in different industries (as in the case of isopropyl alcohol sold directly to manufacturers or indirectly to them via distributors) clearly focuses attention, responsibility, and effort. Companies that organize their marketing this way generally have a clear competitive advantage.

The list of highly differentiated consumer products that not long ago were sold as undifferentiated or minimally differentiated commodities is long: coffee, soap, flour, beer, salt, oatmeal, pickles, frankfurters, bananas, chickens, pineapples, and many more. Among consumer intangibles, in recent years brand or vendor differentiation has intensified in banking, insurance of all kinds, credit cards, stock brokerage, travel agencies, beauty parlors, entertainment parks, and small-loan companies. Among consumer hybrids, the same thing has occurred: theme restaurants, opticians, food retailers, and specialty retailers are burgeoning in a variety of categories— jewelry, sporting goods, books, health and beauty aids, pants and jeans, musical records and cassettes, auto supplies, and home improvement centers.

In each of these cases, especially that of consumer tangibles, the presumption among the less informed is that their competitive distinction resides largely in packaging and advertising. Even substantive differences in the generic products are thought to be so slight that what really counts is the ads and the packages.

This presumption is palpably wrong. It is not simply the heavy advertising or the clever packaging that accounts for the preeminence of so many General Foods and Procter & Gamble products. Nor is it their superior generic products that explain the successes of IBM, Xerox, ITT, and Texas Instruments. Their real distinction lies in how they manage—especially, in the cases of P&G, General Foods, IBM, and Xerox, in how they manage marketing. The amount of careful analysis, control, and field work that characterizes their management of marketing is masked by the visibility of their advertising or presumed generic product uniqueness.

The branded food products companies advertise heavily, and they work as hard and as closely with their wholesale and retail distributors as do the auto companies. Indeed, often these food companies work with distributors even harder because their distributors handle many competing brands and the distribution channels are longer and more complex. Most grocery stores, of course, handle a number of more or less competing brands of the same generic (or functionally undifferentiated) product. There are more than two dozen national brands of powdered laundry detergent. The stores get them from a supermarket chain warehouse or from the warehouse of a cooperative wholesaler, a voluntary wholesaler, or an independent wholesaler. Each of these warehouses generally carries a full line of competing brands.

Though the national brands try via advertising and promotion to create consumer "pull," they also try to create retailer and wholesaler "push." At retail they regularly seek more advantageous shelf space and more advertising support from the retailer. At wholesale they do other things. Some years ago General Foods did a massive study of materials handling in distribution warehouses. Then the company made its results and recommendations available to the trade through a crew of specialists carefully trained to help implement those recommendations. The object, obviously, was to curry favor with the distributive trades for General Foods products.

The company did something similar for retailers: it undertook a major study of retail space profitability and then offered supermarket owners the oppor-

The complexity of a generic product

Durum is a variety of wheat produced in rather small quantities and almost exclusively in three counties in eastern North Dakota. Its main use is in pasta. Farmers generally deliver the durum in truckload quantities to country elevators, from which it is shipped to processors. In recent years, however, many large farm operations have built their own storage elevators. Using very large trailer trucks, they make direct shipments to the elevators of large users. Thus they not only avoid middleman storage discounts, but they also obtain access to premiums paid by the purchasers for high-quality wheat.

Similarly, country elevator operators in the Great Plains have increasingly organized to take advantage of unit-train shipments to the Gulf Coast and thereby qualify for substantial rail tariff discounts. These arrangements affect the quantities and schedules by which country elevators prefer to buy and take delivery from growers, which in turn affect how the growers manage their delivery capabilities and schedules.

The prices that elevator operators and processors pay vary substantially, even for identical grades of durum wheat. The elevator operators will pay premiums above, or take discounts from, prices currently quoted or prices previously agreed to with farmers, depending on the results of protein and moisture tests made on each delivery. Wheat users, like Prince Spaghetti Company, make additional tests for farina and gluten content. Premiums and discounts for quality differences in a particular year have been known to vary from the futures prices on commodity exchanges by amounts greater than the futures price fluctuations themselves during that year.

tunity to learn a new way of space-profitability accounting. By helping retailers manage their space better, General Foods presumably would gain retailers' favor for its products in their merchandising activities.

Another company, Pillsbury, devised a program to help convenience stores operate and compete more effectively. The object was, of course, to obtain preferential push treatment for Pillsbury products in these stores.

Similar examples abound in branded food marketing:

☐ The form in which goods are delivered—pallets, dollies, bulk—is often customized.

☐ When Heinz sells, delivers, and packages ketchup to institutional purveyors who supply hospitals, restaurants, hotels, prisons, schools, and nursing homes, it not only operates differently from the way it deals with cooperative wholesalers, but it also seeks to operate in some advantage-producing fashion different from the way Hunt Foods deals with the same purveyors.

☐ Some years ago the Institutional Food Service Division of General Foods provided elaborate theme-

Exhibit II
Presumed results of improved sales distribution

Industry and use	Millions of pounds	Additional cash contributions of incremental price points by price increments per pound		
		$.001	$.002	$.005
Acetone	124	$124,000	$248,000	$ 620,000
Other intermediates	20	20,000	40,000	100,000
Agribiochemical	31	31,000	62,000	155,000
Coatings	86	86,000	172,000	430,000
Other	49	49,000	98,000	245,000
Total	310	$310,000	$620,000	$1,550,000
If 50% had been sold at the premiums		$155,000	$310,000	$ 775,000
If 10% had been sold at the premiums		$ 31,000	$ 62,000	$ 155,000

meal recipes for schools—"safari" meals that included such delectables as "groundnut soup Uganda" and "fish Mozambique." General Foods provided "decorations to help you go native" in the cafeteria, including travel posters, Congo face masks, pith helmets, lotus garlands, and paper monkeys.

Case of isopropanol

Four of the companies I have mentioned before (General Foods, P&G, IBM, Xerox) are organized along product or brand-management lines for their major generic products. IBM and Xerox also have market managers and geographic managers. What differentiates them from others is how well they manage marketing, not merely what they market. It is the *process*, not just the product, that is differentiated.

To see the importance of the process, let's consider the lost opportunities of a company lacking the right process. Take the case of a large manufacturer of isopropyl alcohol, commonly called isopropanol. It is a moderately simple, totally undifferentiated generic product chemically synthesized via a well-known process from gas recovered in petroleum refining. It comes in two grades: crude, which is 9% water, and refined, which is 1% water. In 1970, 1.9 billion pounds were produced in the United States. Of that amount, 43% was bought as a feed stock to make acetone (principally a solvent), and most of the remainder was bought for use in chemicals, lacquers, and protective coatings.

With the introduction of the new cumene process, isopropanol was no longer needed in the manufacturing of acetone. Hence in 1970 isopropanol was

in vast oversupply. Prices were deeply depressed and expected to remain so for some five years until demand caught up with supply. One of the larger isopropanol companies employed a substantial proportion of its output to make acetone. In 1970 the company sold 310 million pounds of both products to the "merchant market"—that is, directly to manufacturers.

Although the prevailing prices per pound for both acetone and isopropanol were exceedingly low (as low as $.04 for acetone and $.067 for isopropanol), later analysis of this producer's invoices showed wide variations around these prices for sales made to different customers even on the same days. Two possible conclusions follow: (1) not all buyers were identically informed about what, indeed, were the "prevailing" prices on each of those days, and (2) not all buyers were equally price sensitive.

Analysis showed further that these price variations tended to cluster by industry category and customer size but not by geographical location. Another breakdown of industry categories revealed still other price segments: manufacturers of various kinds of coatings exhibited different clusterings of prices they had paid. Substantial differences in prices paid also showed up between agricultural chemical producers and biochemical producers. A category called "other" showed a great variety of price clusterings.

All this, however, is a matter of hindsight. No such analysis was made at the time. Had the marketing process been managed well, a product manager would have known these facts. The revealed differences in invoice prices and price clusterings would have led an intelligent and inquisitive product manager to ask:

1. Who are the least price-aware or price-sensitive among the industry users to whom we sell? What is their size distribution? Exactly which companies are they?

2. Who are the most and the least vendor-loyal—that is, who buys regularly from us, regardless of price fluctuations? Why? And who buys from us only occasionally, largely on considerations of price?

3. Who can use our applications help most? Who least?

4. Who would respond most to our offer for help?

5. Where and with whom could we selectively raise prices? Should we selectively hold prices?

6. How should we communicate all this to the sales organization and employ it in managing the sales forces?

Suppose that by astute management, the sales force had sold largely to the less informed or less price-sensitive industry sectors or customers. Suppose that each customer segment had yielded higher prices of as little as $.001, $.002, or $.005 per pound. What would have been the immediate cash contribution to the company? *Exhibit II* gives an answer.

If only 10% of total sales had been made for only one-tenth of a penny more than they were, the pre-tax contribution would have risen $31,000. If 50% of sales had been raised by this minuscule amount, the yield would have been an extra $155,000; if 50% had been raised by two-tenths of a penny, the yield would have been $310,000 extra.

Given the analysis of markets and users that I outlined, such increases seem to have been well within reach. To get them, how much would it have been worth to expand the market analysis function into an on-the-spot, on-line differentiating activity guiding the sales organization? Obviously, a lot.

It is this and related kinds of attention to marketing details that characterize the work of product managers and market managers. Among producers of generically undifferentiated products—particularly of products sold as ingredients to industrial customers—the management of the marketing process can itself be a powerful differentiating device. This device is constantly and assiduously employed in the better-managed branded, packaged consumer goods companies.

It is a matter of staying aware of exactly what's going on in the market, of how people use, misuse, or modify their products, of how and where they buy, of who makes buying decisions and how these get modified, and the like. It is a matter of looking continuously for gaps in market coverage that the company can fill, of looking continuously at new ways of influencing buyers to choose one's product instead of a competitor's. In this unceasing effort of the manager, *the way in which he operates* becomes an extension of the idea of product differentiation itself.

While differentiation is most readily apparent in branded, packaged consumer goods, in the design, operating character, or composition of industrial goods, or in the features or "service" intensity of intangible products, differentiation consists as powerfully in how one operates the business. In the way the marketing process is managed may reside the opportunity for many companies, especially those that offer generically undifferentiated products and services, to escape the commodity trap.▽

Reprint 80107

Marketing intangible products and product intangibles

Giving tangibility to imperceptible product features can aid both sales and postsales efforts

Theodore Levitt

All products, whether they are services or goods, possess a certain amount of intangibility. Services like insurance and transportation, of course, are nearly entirely intangible. And even goods, while they can be seen, often can't be tried out before they are bought. Understanding the degree of a product's intangibility can affect both sales and postsales follow-up strategies. While services are less able to be tested in advance than goods, the intangible factors in both types of products are important for convincing prospective customers to buy. Sellers of services, however, face special problems in making customers aware of the benefits they are receiving. The author considers the intangible factors present in all products and also advises producers of services about how best to hold on to their customers.

Mr. Levitt is the Edward W. Carter Professor of Business Administration and head of the marketing area at the Harvard Business School. He has written nearly two dozen articles for HBR, including the well-known "Marketing Myopia" (published in 1960 and reprinted as an HBR Classic in September-October 1975) and "Marketing When Things Change" (November-December 1977).

Illustration by Jim Kingston.

Distinguishing between companies according to whether they market services or goods has only limited utility. A more useful way to make the same distinction is to change the words we use. Instead of speaking of *services* and *goods*, we should speak of *intangibles* and *tangibles*. Everybody sells intangibles in the marketplace, no matter what is produced in the factory.

The usefulness of the distinction becomes apparent when we consider the question of how the marketing of intangibles differs from the marketing of tangibles. While some of the differences might seem obvious, it is apparent that, along with their differences, there are important commonalities between the marketing of intangibles and tangibles.

Put in terms of our new vocabulary, a key area of similarity in the marketing of intangibles and tangibles revolves around the degree of intangibility inherent in both. Marketing is concerned with getting and keeping customers. The degree of product intangibility has its greatest effect in the process of trying to get customers. When it comes to holding on to customers—to keeping them—highly intangible products run into very special problems.

First, this article identifies aspects of intangibility that affect sales appeal of both intangible and tangible products. And, next, it considers the special

Author's note: The current article expands on and further develops some of the concepts I introduced in my last article for HBR, "Marketing Success Through Differentiation—Of Anything," which appeared in the January-February 1980 issue. Other articles I have written for HBR treat this general subject in yet other ways. These include "The Industrialization of Service" (September-October 1976) and "Production-Line Approach to Service" (September-October 1972). To drive home what I believe is a badly neglected distinction, the present article refers to the role of management in the industrial revolution, a subject more fully developed in my article, "Management and Post Industrial Society," *The Public Interest,* Summer 1976.

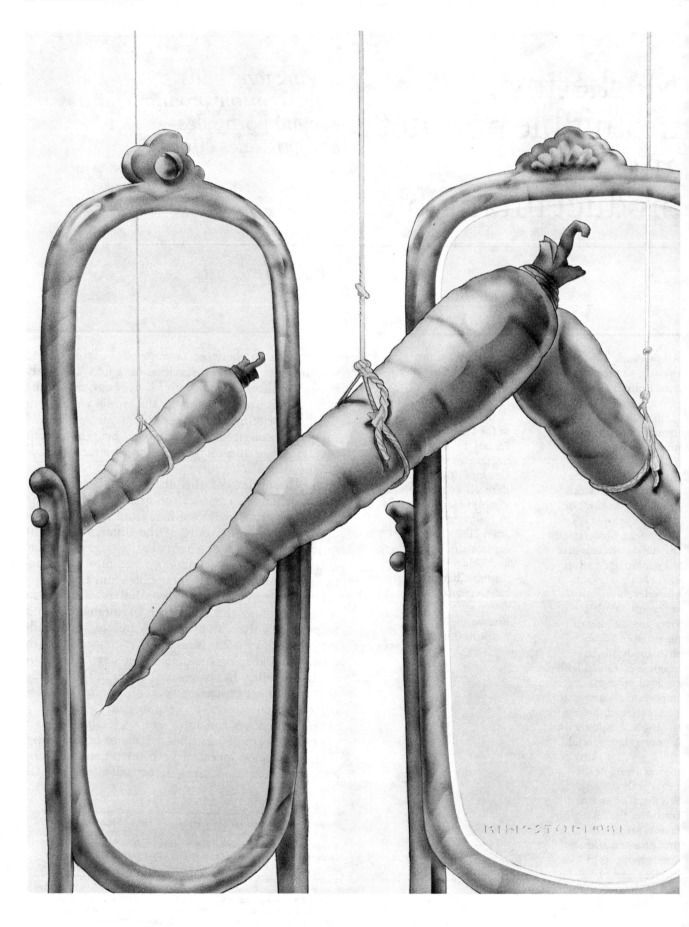

difficulties sellers of intangibles face in retaining customers.

Intangibility of all products

Intangible products—travel, freight forwarding, insurance, repair, consulting, computer software, investment banking, brokerage, education, health care, accounting—can seldom be tried out, inspected, or tested in advance. Prospective buyers are generally forced to depend on surrogates to assess what they're likely to get.

They can look at gloriously glossy pictures of elegant rooms in distant resort hotels set exotically by the shimmering sea. They can consult current users to see how well a software program performs and how well the investment banker or the oil well drilling contractor performs. Or they can ask experienced customers regarding engineering firms, trust companies, lobbyists, professors, surgeons, prep schools, hair stylists, consultants, repair shops, industrial maintenance firms, shippers, franchisers, general contractors, funeral directors, caterers, environmental management firms, construction companies, and on and on.

Tangible products differ in that they can usually, or to some degree, be directly experienced—seen, touched, smelled, or tasted, as well as tested. Often this can be done in advance of buying. You can test-drive a car, smell the perfume, work the numerical controls of a milling machine, inspect the seller's steam-generating installation, pretest an extruding machine.

In practice, though, even the most tangible of products can't be *reliably* tested or experienced in advance. To inspect a vendor's steam-generating plant or computer installation in advance at another location and to have thoroughly studied detailed proposals and designs are not enough. A great deal more is involved than product features and physical installation alone.

Though a customer may buy a product whose generic tangibility (like the computer or the steam plant) is as palpable as primeval rock—and though that customer may have agreed after great study and extensive negotiation to a cost that runs into millions of dollars—the process of getting it built on time, installed, and then running smoothly involves an awful lot more than the generic tangible product itself. Such intangibles can make or break the product's success, even with mature consumer goods like dishwashers, shampoos, and frozen pizza. If a shampoo is not used as prescribed, or a pizza not heated as intended, the results can be terrible.

Similarly, you commonly can't experience in advance moderate-to-low-priced consumer goods such as canned sardines or purchased detergents. To make buyers more comfortable and confident about tangibles that can't be pretested, companies go beyond the literal promises of specifications, advertisements, and labels to provide reassurance.

Packaging is one common tool. Pickles get put into reassuring see-through glass jars, cookies into cellophane-windowed boxes, canned goods get strong appetite-appealing pictures on the labels, architects make elaborately enticing renderings, and proposals to NASA get packaged in binders that match the craftsmanship of Tyrolean leatherworkers. In all cases, the idea is to provide reassuring tangible (in these examples, visual) surrogates for what's promised but can't be more directly experienced before the sale.

Hence, it's sensible to say that all products are in some important respects intangible, even giant turbine engines that weigh tons. No matter how diligently designed in advance and carefully constructed, they'll fail or disappoint if installed or used incorrectly. The significance of all this for marketing can be profound.

When prospective customers can't experience the product in advance, they are asked to buy what are essentially promises—promises of satisfaction. Even tangible, testable, feelable, smellable products are, before they're bought, largely just promises.

Buying promises

Satisfaction in consumption or use can seldom be quite the same as earlier in trial or promise. Some promises promise more than others, depending on product features, design, degree of tangibility, type of promotion, price, and differences in what customers hope to accomplish with what they buy.

Of some products less is expected than what is actually or symbolically promised. The right kind of eye shadow properly applied may promise to transform a woman into an irresistible tigress in the night. Not even the most eager buyer literally believes the metaphor. Yet the metaphor helps make the sale. Neither do you really expect the proposed new corporate headquarters, so artfully rendered by the winning architect, automatically to produce all those cheerfully productive employees lounging with casual elegance at lunch in the verdant courtyard. But the metaphor helps win the assignment.

Thus, when prospective customers can't properly try the promised product in advance, metaphorical reassurances become the amplified necessity of the marketing effort. Promises, being intangible, have to be "tangibilized" in their presentation—hence the tigress and the contented employees. Metaphors and similes become surrogates for the tangibility that cannot be provided or experienced in advance.

This same thinking accounts for the solid, somber Edwardian decor of downtown law offices, the prudentially elegant and orderly public offices of investment banking houses, the confidently articulate consultants in dark vested suits, engineering and project proposals in "executive" typeset and leather bindings, and the elaborate pictorial documentation of the performance virtuosity of newly offered machine controls. It explains why insurance companies pictorially offer "a piece of the rock," put you under a "blanket of protection" or an "umbrella," or place you in "good hands."

Not even tangible products are exempt from the necessity of using symbol and metaphor. A computer terminal has to look right. It has to be packaged to convey an impression of reliable modernity—based on the assumption that prospective buyers will translate appearance into confidence about performance. In that respect, the marketing ideas behind the packaging of a $1 million computer, a $2 million jet engine, and a $.5 million numerically controlled milling machine are scarcely different from the marketing ideas behind the packaging of a $50 electric shaver or a $2.50 tube of lipstick.

Importance of impressions

Common sense tells us, and research confirms, that people use appearances to make judgments about realities. It matters little whether the products are high priced or low priced, whether they are technically complex or simple, whether the buyers are supremely sophisticated in the technology of what's being considered or just plain ignorant, or whether they buy for themselves or for their employers. Everybody always depends to some extent on both appearances and external impressions.

Nor do impressions affect only the generic product itself—that is, the technical offering, such as the speed, versatility, and precision of the lathe; the color and creaminess of the lipstick; or the appearance and dimensions of the lobster thermidor. Con-

sider, for example, investment banking. No matter how thorough and persuasive a firm's recommendations and assurances about a proposed underwriting and no matter how pristine its reputation for integrity and performance, somehow the financial vice president of the billion-dollar client corporation would feel better had the bank's representative not been quite so youthfully apple-cheeked.

The product will be judged in part by who offers it—not just who the vendor corporation is but also who the corporation's representative is. The vendor and the vendor's representative are both inextricably and inevitably part of the "product" that prospects must judge before they buy. The less tangible the generic product, the more powerfully and persistently the judgment about it gets shaped by the packaging—how it's presented, who presents it, and what's implied by metaphor, simile, symbol, and other surrogates for reality.

So, too, with tangible products. The sales engineers assigned to work with an electric utility company asking for competitive bids on a $100 million steam boiler system for its new plant are as powerfully a part of the offered product (the promise) as is the investment banking firm's partner.

The reason is easy to see. In neither case is there a product until it's delivered. And you won't know how well it performs until it's put to work.

The ties that bind

In both investment banking and big boilers, becoming the designated vendor requires successful passage through several consecutive gates, or stages, in the sales process. It is not unlike courtship. Both "customers" know that a rocky courtship spells trouble ahead. If the groom is not sufficiently solicitous during the courtship—if he's insensitive to moods and needs, unresponsive or wavering during stress or adversity—there will be problems in the marriage.

But unlike a real marriage, investment banking and installed boiler systems allow no room for divorce. Once the deal is made, marriage and gestation have simultaneously begun. After that, things are often irreversible. Investment banking may require months of close work with the client organization before the underwriting can be launched—that is, before the baby is born. And the construction of an electric power plant takes years, through sickness and in health. As with babies, birth of any kind presents new problems. Babies have to be coddled to see them through early life. Illness or relapse has to be conscientiously avoided or quickly corrected.

Similarly, stocks or bonds should not go quickly to deep discounts. The boiler should not suddenly malfunction after several weeks or months. If it does, it should be rapidly restored to full use. Understandably, the prospective customer will, in courtship, note every nuance carefully, judging always what kind of a husband and father the eager groom is likely to make.

The way the product is packaged (how the promise is presented in brochure, letter, design appearance), how it is personally presented, and by whom —all these become central to the product itself because they are elements of what the customer finally decides to buy or reject.

A product is more than a tangible thing, even a $100 million boiler system. From a buyer's viewpoint, the product is a promise, a cluster of value expectations of which its nontangible qualities are as integral as its tangible parts. Certain conditions must be satisfied before the prospect buys. If they are not satisfied, there is no sale. There would have been no sale in the cases of the investment banker and the boiler manufacturer if, during the prebidding (or courtship) stages of the relationship, their representatives had been improperly responsive to or insufficiently informed about the customers' special situations and problems.

In each case, the promised product—the whole product—would have been unsatisfactory. It is not that it would have been incomplete; it just would not have been right. Changing the salespeople in midstream probably would not have helped, since the selling organization would by then have already "said" the wrong thing about its "product." If, during the courtship, the prospective customer got the impression that there might be aftermarket problems—problems in execution, in timeliness, in the postsale support necessary for smooth and congenial relations—then the customer would have received a clear message that the delivered product would be faulty.

Special problems for intangibles

So much, briefly, for making a sale—for getting a customer. *Keeping* a customer is quite another thing, and on that score more pervasively intangible products encounter some distinct difficulties.

These difficulties stem largely from the fact that intangible products are highly people-intensive in their production and delivery methods. Corporate financial services of banks are, in this respect, not so different from hairdressing or consulting. The more people-intensive a product, the more room there is for personal discretion, idiosyncracy, error, and delay. Once a customer for an intangible product is sold, the customer can easily be unsold as a consequence of the underfulfillment of his expectations. Repeat buying suffers. Conversely, a tangible product, manufactured under close supervision in a factory and delivered through a planned and orderly network, is much more likely than an intangible product to fulfill the promised expectation. Repeat buying is therefore less easily jeopardized.

A tangible product is usually developed by design professionals working under conditions of benign isolation after receiving guidance from market intelligence experts, scientists, and others. The product will be manufactured by another group of specialists under conditions of close supervision that facilitate reliable quality control. Even installation and use by the customer are determined by a relatively narrow range of possibilities dictated by the product itself.

Intangible products present an entirely different picture. Consider a computer software program. The programmer does the required research directly and generally on the customer's premises, trying to understand complex networks of interconnecting operations. Then that same person designs the system and the software, usually alone. The process of designing is, simultaneously, also the process of manufacturing. Design and manufacturing of intangible products are generally done by the same people— or by one person alone, like a craftsman at a bench.

Moreover, manufacturing an intangible product is generally indistinguishable from its actual delivery. In situations such as consulting, the delivery *is* the manufacturing from the client's viewpoint. Though the consulting study may have been excellent, if the delivery is poor, the study will be viewed as having been badly manufactured. It's a faulty product. So too with the work of all types of brokers, educators and trainers, accounting firms, engineering firms, architects, lawyers, transportation companies, hospitals and clinics, government agencies, banks, trust companies, mutual funds, car rental companies, insurance companies, repair and maintenance operations, and on and on. For each, delivery and production are virtually indistinguishable. The whole difference is nicely summarized by Professor John M. Rathwell of Cornell University: "Goods are produced, services are performed." [1]

---

1. John M. Rathwell, *Marketing in the Service Sector* (Cambridge, Mass.: Winthrop Publishers, 1974), p. 58.

Minimizing the human factor

Because companies making intangible products are highly people-intensive operations, they have an enormous quality control problem. Quality control on an automobile assembly line is built into the system. If a yellow door is hung on a red car, somebody on the line will quickly ask if that's what was intended. If the left front wheel is missing, the person next in line, whose task is to fasten the lug bolts, will stop the line. But if a commercial banker misses an important feature of a financing package or if he doesn't do it well, it may never be found—or found too late. If the ashtrays aren't cleaned on a rented car, that discovery will annoy or irritate the already committed customer. Repeat business gets jeopardized.

No matter how well trained or motivated they might be, people make mistakes, forget, commit indiscretions, and at times are uncongenial—hence the search for alternatives to dependence on people. Previously in HBR, I have suggested a variety of ways to reduce people dependence in the so-called service industries. I called it the *industrialization of service*, which means substituting hard, soft, or hybrid technologies for totally people-intensive activities:

☐ *Hard* technologies include automatic telephone dialing for operator-assisted dialing, credit cards for repetitive credit checking, and computerized monitoring of industrial processes. And the benefits are considerable. Automatic telephone switching is, for example, not only cheaper than manual switching but far more reliable.

☐ *Soft* technologies are the substitution of division of labor for one-person craftsmanship in production—as, for example, organizing the work force that cleans an office building so that each worker specializes in one or several limited tasks (dusting, waxing, vacuuming, window cleaning) rather than each person doing all these jobs alone. Insurance companies long ago went to extensive division of labor in their applications processing—registering, underwriting, performing actuarial functions, issuing policies.

☐ *Hybrid* technologies combine the soft and the hard. The floor is waxed by a machine rather than by hand. French fries are precut and portion packed in a factory for finishing in a fast-food restaurant in specially designed deep fryers that signal when the food is ready. A computer automatically calculates and makes all entries in an Internal Revenue Service form 1040 after a moderately trained clerk has entered the raw data on a console.

The managerial revolution

Industrializing helps control quality and cut costs. Instead of depending on people to work *better*, industrialization redesigns the work so that people work *differently*. Thus, the same modes of managerial rationality are applied to service—the production, creation, and delivery of largely intangible products—that were first applied to production of goods in the nineteenth century. The real significance of the nineteenth century is not the industrial revolution, with its shift from animal to machine power, but rather the managerial revolution, with its shift from the craftsman's functional independence to the manager's rational routines.

In successive waves, the mechanical harvester, the sewing machine, and then the automobile epitomized the genius of that century. Each was rationally designed to become an assembled rather than a constructed machine, a machine that depended not on the idiosyncratic artistry of a single craftsman but on simple, standardized tasks performed on routine specifications by unskilled workers. This required detailed managerial planning to ensure proper design, manufacture, and assembly of interchangeable parts so that the right number of people would be at the right places at the right times to do the right simple jobs in the right ways. Then, with massive output, distribution, and after-market training and service, managers had to create and maintain systems to justify the massive output.

On being appreciated

What's been largely missing in intangible goods production is the kind of managerial rationality that produced the industrial revolution. That is why the quality of intangibles tends to be less reliable than it might be, costs higher than they should be, and customer satisfaction lower than it need be.

While I have referred to the enormous progress that has in recent years been made on these matters, there is one characteristic of intangible products that requires special attention for holding customers. Unique to intangible products is the fact that the customer is seldom aware of being served well. This is especially so in the case of intangible products that have, for the duration of the contract, constant continuity—that is, you're buying or using or consuming them almost constantly. Such products include certain banking services, cleaning services, freight hauling, energy management, maintenance services, telephones, and the like.

Consider an international banking relationship, an insurance relationship, an industrial cleaning relationship. If all goes well, the customer is virtually oblivious to what he's getting. Only when things don't go well (or a competitor says they don't) does the customer become aware of the product's existence or nonexistence—when a letter of credit is incorrectly drawn, when a competitive bank proposes better arrangements, when the annual insurance premium notice arrives or when a claim is disputed, when the ashtrays aren't cleaned, or when a favorite penholder is missing.

The most important thing to know about intangible products is that the *customers usually don't know what they're getting until they don't get it.* Only then do they become aware of what they bargained for; only on dissatisfaction do they dwell. Satisfaction is, as it should be, mute. Its existence is affirmed only by its absence.

And that's dangerous—because the customers will be aware only of failure and of dissatisfaction, not of success or satisfaction. That makes them terribly vulnerable to the blandishments of competitive sellers. A competitor can always structure a more interesting corporate financing deal, always propose a more imaginative insurance program, always find dust on top of the framed picture in the office, always cite small visible failures that imply big hidden ones.

In getting customers for intangibles it is important to create surrogates, or metaphors, for tangibility—how we dress; how we articulate, write, design, and present proposals; how we work with prospects, respond to inquiries, and initiate ideas; and how well we show we understand the prospect's business. But in keeping customers for intangibles, it becomes important regularly to remind and show them what they're getting so that occasional failures fade in relative importance. If that's not done, the customers will not know. They'll only know when they're *not* getting what they bought, and that's all that's likely to count.

To keep customers for regularly delivered and consumed intangible products, again, they have to be reminded of what they're getting. Vendors must regularly reinstate the promises that were made to land the customer. Thus, when an insurance prospect finally gets "married," the subsequent silence and inattention can be deafening. Most customers seldom recall for long what kind of life insurance package they bought, often forgetting as well the name of both underwriter and agent. To be reminded a year later via a premium notice often brings to mind the contrast between the loving at-

tention of courtship and the cold reality of marriage. No wonder the lapse rate in personal life insurance is so high!

Once a relationship is cemented, the seller has created equity. He has a customer. To help keep the customer, the seller must regularly enhance the equity in that relationship lest it decline and become jeopardized by competitors.

There are innumerable ways to do that strengthening, and some of these can be systematized, or industrialized. Periodic letters or phone calls that remind the customer of how well things are going cost little and are surprisingly powerful equity maintainers. Newsletters or regular visits suggesting new, better, or augmented product features are useful. Even nonbusiness socializing has its value— as is affirmed by corporations struggling in recent years with the IRS about the deductibility of hunting lodges, yachts, clubs, and spouses attending conferences and customer meetings.

Here are some examples of how companies have strengthened their relationships with customers:

☐ An energy management company sends out a periodic "Update Report" on conspicuous yellow paper, advising clients how to discover and correct energy leaks, install improved monitors, and accomplish cost savings.

☐ A computer service bureau organizes its account managers for a two-week series of blitz customer callbacks to "explain casually" the installation of new central processing equipment that is expected to prevent cost increases next year while expanding the customers' interactive options.

☐ A long-distance hauler of high-value electronic equipment (computers, terminals, mail sorters, word processors, medical diagnostic instruments) has instituted quarterly performance reviews with its shippers, some of which include customers who are encouraged to talk about their experiences and expectations.

☐ An insurance company sends periodic one-page notices to policyholders *and* policy beneficiaries. These generally begin with a single-sentence congratulation that policy and coverage remain nicely intact and follow with brief views on recent tax rulings affecting insurance, new notions about personal financial planning, and special protection packages available with other types of insurance.

In all these ways, sellers of intangible products reinstate their presence and performance in the customers' minds, reminding them of their continuing presence and the value of what is constantly, and silently, being delivered.

Making tangible the intangible

It bears repeating that all products have elements of tangibility and intangibility. Companies that sell tangible products invariably promise more than the tangible products themselves. Indeed, enormous efforts often focus on the enhancement of the intangibles—promises of bountiful benefits conferred rather than on features offered. To the buyer of photographic film, Kodak promises with unremitting emphasis the satisfactions of enduring remembrance, of memories clearly preserved. Kodak says almost nothing about the superior luminescence of its pictures. The product is thus remembrance, not film or pictures.

The promoted products of the automobile, as everyone knows, are largely status, comfort, and power—intangible things of the mind, rather than tangible things from the factory. Auto dealers, on the other hand, assuming correctly that people's minds have already been reached by the manufacturers' ads, focus on other considerations: deals, availability, and postpurchase servicing. Neither the dealers nor the manufacturers sell the tangible cars themselves. Rather, they sell the intangible benefits that are bundled into the entire package.

If tangible products must be intangibilized to add customer-getting appeal, then intangible products must be tangibilized—what Professor Leonard L. Berry calls "managing the evidence."[2] Ideally, this should be done as a matter of routine on a systematic basis—that is, industrialized. For instance, hotels wrap their drinking glasses in fresh bags or film, put on the toilet seat a "sanitized" paper band, and neatly shape the end piece of the toilet tissue into a fresh-looking arrowhead. All these actions say with silent affirmative clarity that "the room has been specially cleaned for your use and comfort"—yet no words are spoken to say it. Words, in any case, would be less convincing, nor could employees be reliably depended on to say them each time or to say them convincingly. Hotels have thus not only tangibilized their promise, they've also industrialized its delivery.

Or take the instructive case of purchasing house insulation, which most home owners approach with understandable apprehension. Suppose you call two companies to bid on installing insulation in your house. The first insulation installer arrives in a car. After pacing once around the house with mea-

sured self-assurance and after quick calculations on the back of an envelope, there comes a confident quote of $2,400 for six-inch fiberglass—total satisfaction guaranteed.

Another drives up in a clean white truck with clipboard in hand and proceeds to scrupulously measure the house dimensions, count the windows, crawl the attic, and consult records from a source book on the area's seasonal temperature ranges and wind velocities. The installer then asks a host of questions, meanwhile recording everything with obvious diligence. There follows a promise to return in three days, which happens at the appointed hour, with a typed proposal for six-inch fiberglass insulation at $2,800—total satisfaction guaranteed. From which company will you buy?

The latter has tangibilized the intangible, made a promise into a credible expectation. Even more persuasive tangible evidence is provided by an insulation supplier whose representative types the relevant information into a portable intelligent printing terminal. The analysis and response are almost instant, causing one user to call it "the most powerful tool ever developed in the insulation industry." If the house owner is head of a project buying team of an electric utility company, the treasurer of a mighty corporation, the materials purchasing agent of a ready-mixed cement company, the transportation manager of a fertilizer manufacturer, or the data processing director of an insurance company, it's almost certain this person will make vendor decisions at work in the same way as around the house. Everybody requires the risk-reducing reassurances of tangibilized intangibles.

Managers can use the practice of providing reassuring ways to render tangible the intangible's promises—even when the generic product is itself tangible. Laundry detergents that claim special whitening capabilities lend credibility to the promise by using "blue whitener beads" that are clearly visible to the user. Procter & Gamble's new decaffeinated instant coffee, "High Point," reinforces the notion of real coffee with luminescent "milled flakes for hearty, robust flavor." You can *see* what the claims promise.

Keeping customers for an intangible product requires constant reselling efforts while things go well lest the customer get lost when things go badly. The reselling requires that tasks be industrialized. The relationship with the customer must be managed much more carefully and continuously in the case of intangibles than of tangible products, though it is vital in both. And it gets progressively more vital

2. Leonard L. Berry, "Service Marketing Is Different," *Business*, May-June 1980, p. 24. He is with the University of Virginia, Charlottesville.

for tangible products that are new and especially complex. In such cases, "relationship management" becomes a special art—another topic all its own.

Meanwhile, the importance of what I've tried to say here is emphasized by one overriding fact: a customer is an asset usually more precious than the tangible assets on the balance sheet. Balance sheet assets can generally be bought. There are lots of willing sellers. Customers cannot so easily be bought. Lots of eager sellers are offering them many choices. Moreover, a customer is a double asset. First, the customer is the direct source of cash from the sale and, second, the existence of a solid customer can be used to raise cash from bankers and investors—cash that can be converted into tangible assets.

The old chestnut "nothing happens till you make a sale" is awfully close to an important truth. What it increasingly takes to make and keep that sale is to tangibilize the intangible, restate the benefit and source to the customer, and industrialize the processes.▽

Reprint 81306

Service Marketing

Harvard
Business Review

Theodore Levitt

Production-line approach to service

Once service 'in the field' receives the same
attention as products 'in the factory,'
a lot of new opportunities become possible

Foreword

We think about service in humanistic terms; we think about manufacturing in technocratic terms. This, according to the author, is why manufacturing industries are forward-looking and efficient while service industries and customer service are, by comparison, primitive and inefficient. He argues that if companies stop thinking of service as servitude and personal ministration, they will be able to effect drastic improvements in its quality and efficiency. Then he shows companies how to take a manufacturing approach to this activity, one that substitutes "technology and systems for people and serendipity."

Mr. Levitt is Professor of Business Administration at the Harvard Business School, and a familiar author to HBR readers. His articles have won three McKinsey awards and a John Hancock Award for Excellence. His most recent book is *The Marketing Mode* (New York, McGraw-Hill, 1969).

The service sector of the economy is growing in size but shrinking in quality. So say a lot of people. Purveyors of service, for their part, think that they and their problems are fundamentally different from other businesses and their prob-lems. They feel that service is people-intensive, while the rest of the economy is capital-intensive. But these distinctions are largely spurious. There are no such things as service indus-tries. There are only industries whose service components are greater or less than those of other industries. Everybody is in service.

Often the less there seems, the more there is. The more technologically sophisticated the generic product (e.g., cars and computers), the more dependent are its sales on the quality and availability of its accompanying customer services (e.g., display rooms, delivery, repairs and maintenance, application aids, operator training, installation advice, warranty fulfillment). In this sense, General Motors is probably more service-intensive than manufacturing-intensive. Without its services its sales would shrivel.

Thus the service sector of the economy is not merely comprised of the so-called service industries, such as banking, airlines, and maintenance. It includes the entire abundance of product-related services supplied by manufacturers and the sales-related services supplied by retailers. Yet we confuse things to our detriment by an outdated taxonomy. For example:

☐ The First National City Bank (Citibank) is one of the biggest worldwide banks. It has about 37,000 employees, over half of whom deal directly with the public, either selling them things (mostly money and deposit services) or helping them with things they have already bought (cashing checks, taking additional deposits, writing letters of credit, opening lockboxes, managing corporate cash). Most of the other employees work back in what is called "the factory" —a massive congeries of people, paper, and computers that processes, records, validates, and scrutinizes everything the first group has done. All the corporate taxonomists, including the U.S. Department of the Census, classify Citibank as a service company.

☐ IBM is the biggest worldwide manufacturer of computers. It has about 270,000 employees, over half of whom deal directly with the public, either selling them things (mostly machines) or helping them with the things they have already bought (installing and repairing machines, writing computer programs, training customers). Most of the other employees work back in the factory—a massive congeries of wires, microminiature electronic components, engineers, and assemblers. All the corporate taxonomists, including the U.S. Department of the Census, classify IBM as a manufacturing company.

Something is wrong, and not just in the Bureau of the Census. The industrial world has changed more rapidly than our taxonomies. If only taxonomy were involved, the consequences of our contradictory classifications would be trivial. After all, man lives perfectly well with his contradictions: his simultaneous faith, for instance, in both God and science; his attachment to facts and logic when making important business decisions, but reliance on feelings and emotion when making far more important life decisions, like marriage.

I hope to show in this article that our contradictory notions about service may have malignant consequences. Not until we clarify the contradictions will companies begin to solve problems that now seem so intractible. In order to do so, they must think of themselves as performing manufacturing functions when it comes to their so-called "service" activities. Only then will they begin to make some significant progress in improving the quality and efficiency of service in the modern economy.

Field versus factory

People think of service as quite different from manufacturing. Service is presumed to be performed by individuals for other individuals, generally on a one-to-one basis. Manufacturing is presumed to be performed by machines, generally tended by large clusters of individuals whose sizes and configurations are themselves dictated by the machines' requirements. Service (whether customer service or the services of service industries) is performed "out there in the field" by distant and loosely supervised people working under highly variable, and often volatile, conditions. Manufacturing occurs "here in the factory" under highly centralized, carefully organized, tightly controlled, and elaborately engineered conditions.

People assume, and rightly so, that these differences largely explain why products produced in the factory are generally more uniform in features and quality than the services produced (e.g., life insurance policies, machine repairs) or delivered (e.g., spare parts, milk) in the field. One cannot as easily control one's agents or their performance out there in the field. Besides, different customers want different things. The result is that service and service industries, in comparison with manufacturing industries, are widely and correctly viewed as being primitive, sluggish, and inefficient.

Yet it is doubtful that things need be all that bad. Once conditions in the field get the same kind of attention that conditions inside the factory generally get, a lot of new opportunities become possible. But first management will have to revise its thinking about what service is and what it implies.

Limits of servitude

The trouble with thinking of oneself as providing services—either in the service industries or in the customer-service sectors of manufacturing and retailing companies—is that one almost inescapably embraces ancient, pre-industrial modes of thinking. Worse still, one gets caught up in rigid attitudes that can have a profoundly paralyzing effect on even the most resolute of rationalists.

The concept of "service" evokes, from the opaque recesses of the mind, time-worn images of personal ministration and attendance. It refers generally to deeds one individual performs personally for another. It carries historical connotations of charity, gallantry, and selflessness, or of obedience, subordination, and subjugation. In these contexts, people serve because they want to (as in the priestly and political professions) or they serve because they are compelled to (as in slavery and such occupations of attendance as waiter, maid, bellboy, cleaning lady).

In the higher-status service occupations, such as in the church and the army, one customarily behaves ritualistically, not rationally. In the lower-status service occupations, one simply obeys. In neither is independent thinking presumed to be a requisite of holding a job. The most that can therefore be expected from service improvements is that, like Avis, a person will try harder. He will just exert more animal effort to do better what he is already doing.

So it was in ancient times, and so it is today. The only difference is that where ancient masters invoked the will of God or the whip of the foreman to spur performance, modern industry uses training programs and motivation sessions. We have not in all these years come very far in either our methods or our results. In short, service thinks humanistically, and that explains its failures.

Promise of manufacturing

Now consider manufacturing. Here the orientation is toward the efficient production of results, not toward attendance on others. Relationships are strictly businesslike, devoid of invidious connotations of rank or self.

When we think about how to improve manufacturing, we seldom focus on ways to improve our personal performance of present tasks; rather, it is axiomatic that we try to find entirely new ways of performing present tasks and, better yet, of actually changing the tasks themselves. We do not think of greater exertion of our animal energies (working physically harder, as the slave), of greater expansion of our commitment (being more devout or loyal, as the priest), or of greater assertion of our dependence (being more obsequious, as the butler).

Instead, we apply the greater exertion of our minds to learn how to look at a problem differently. More particularly, we ask what kinds of tools, old or new, and what kinds of skills, processes, organizational rearrangements, incentives, controls, and audits might be enlisted to greatly improve the intended outcomes. In short, manufacturing thinks technocratically, and that explains its successes.

Manufacturing looks for solutions inside the very tasks to be done. The solution to building a low-priced automobile, for example, derives largely from the nature and composition of the automobile itself. (If the automobile were not an assembly of parts, it could not be manufactured on an assembly line.) By contrast, service looks for solutions in the *performer* of the task. This is the paralyzing legacy of our inherited attitudes: the solution to improved service is viewed as being dependent on improvements in the skills and attitudes of the performers of that service.

While it may pain and offend us to say so, thinking in humanistic rather than technocratic terms ensures that the service sector of the modern economy will be forever inefficient and that our satisfactions will be forever marginal. We see service as invariably and undeviatingly personal, as something performed by individuals directly for other individuals.

This humanistic conception of service diverts us from seeking alternatives to the use of people, especially to large, organized groups of people. It does not allow us to reach out for new solutions and new definitions. It obstructs us from redesigning the tasks themselves; from creating new tools, processes, and organizations; and, perhaps, even from eliminating the conditions that created the problems.

In sum, to improve the quality and efficiency of service, companies must apply the kind of technocratic thinking which in other fields has replaced the high-cost and erratic elegance of the artisan with the low-cost, predictable munificence of the manufacturer.

The technocratic hamburger

Nowhere in the entire service sector are the possibilities of the manufacturing mode of thinking better illustrated than in fast-food franchising. Nowhere have manufacturing methods been employed more effectively to control the operation of distant and independent agents. Nowhere is "service" better.

Few of today's successful new commercial ventures have antecedents that are more humble and less glamorous than the hamburger. Yet the thriving nationwide chain of hamburger stands called "McDonald's" is a supreme example of the application of manufacturing and technological brilliance to problems that must ultimately be viewed as marketing problems. From 1961 to 1970, McDonald's sales rose from approximately $54 million to $587 million. During this remarkable ascent, the White Tower chain, whose name had theretofore been practically synonymous throughout the land with low-priced, quick-service hamburgers, practically vanished.

The explanation of McDonald's thundering success is not a purely fiscal one—i.e., the argument that it is financed by independent local entrepreneurs who bring to their operations a quality of commitment and energy not commonly found among hired workers. Nor is it a purely geographical one—i.e., the argument that each outlet draws its patronage from a relatively small geographic ring of customers, thus enabling the number of outlets easily and quickly to multiply. The relevant explanation must deal with the central question of why each separate McDonald's outlet is so predictably successful, why each is so certain to attract many repeat customers.

Entrepreneurial financing and careful site selection do help. But most important is the carefully controlled execution of each outlet's central function—the rapid delivery of a uniform, high-quality mix of prepared foods in an environment of obvious cleanliness, order, and cheerful courtesy. The systematic substitution of equipment for people, combined with the carefully planned use and positioning of technology, enables McDonald's to attract and hold patronage in proportions no predecessor or imitator has managed to duplicate. Consider the remarkable ingenuity of the system, which is worth examining in some detail:

To start with the obvious, raw hamburger patties are carefully prepacked and premeasured, which leaves neither the franchisee nor his employees any discretion as to size, quality, or raw-material consistency. This kind of attention is given to all McDonald's products. Storage and preparation space and related facilities are expressly designed for, and limited to, the predetermined mix of products. There is no space for any foods, beverages, or services that were not designed into the system at the outset. There is not even a sandwich knife or, in fact, a decent place to keep one. Thus the owner has no discretion regarding what he can sell—not because of any contractual limitations, but because of facilities limitations. And the employees have virtually no discretion regarding how to prepare and serve things.

Discretion is the enemy of order, standardization, and quality. On an automobile assembly line, for example, a worker who has discretion and latitude might possibly produce a more personalized car, but one that is highly unpredictable. The elaborate care with which an automobile is designed and an assembly line is structured and controlled is what produces quality cars at low prices, and with surprising reliability considering the sheer volume of the output. The same is true at McDonald's, which produces food under highly automated and controlled conditions.

French-fried automation

While in Detroit the significance of the technological process lies in production, at McDonald's it lies in marketing. A carefully planned design is built into the elaborate technology of the food-service system in such a fashion as to make it a significant marketing device. This fact is impressively illustrated by McDonald's handling of that uniquely plebeian American delicacy, french-fried potatoes.

French fries become quickly soggy and unappetizing; to be good, they must be freshly made just before serving. Like other fast-food establishments, McDonald's provides its outlets with precut, partially cooked frozen potatoes that can be quickly finished in an on-premises, deep-fry facility. The McDonald's fryer is neither so large that it produces too many french fries at one time (thus allowing them to become soggy) nor so small that it requires frequent and costly frying.

The fryer is emptied onto a wide, flat tray adjacent to the service counter. This location is crucial. Since the McDonald's practice is to create an impression of abundance and generosity by slightly overfilling each bag of french fries, the tray's location next to the service counter prevents the spillage from an overfilled bag from reaching the floor. Spillage creates not only danger underfoot but also an unattractive appearance that causes the employees to become accustomed to an unclean environment. Once a store is unclean in one particular, standards fall very rapidly and the store becomes unclean and the food unappetizing in general.

While McDonald's aims for an impression of abundance, excessive overfilling can be very costly for a company that annually buys potatoes almost by the trainload. A systematic bias that puts into each bag of french fries a half ounce more than is intended can have visible effects on the company's annual earnings. Further, excessive time spent at the tray by each employee can create a cumulative service bottleneck at the counter.

McDonald's has therefore developed a special wide-mouthed scoop with a narrow funnel in its handle. The counter employee picks up the scoop and inserts the handle end into a wall clip containing the bags. One bag adheres to the handle. In a continuous movement the scoop descends into the potatoes, fills the bag to the exact proportions its designers intended, and is lifted, scoop facing the ceiling, so that the potatoes funnel through the handle into the attached bag, which is automatically disengaged from the handle by the weight of the contents. The bag comes to a steady, nonwobbling rest on its flat bottom.

Nothing can go wrong—the employee never soils his hands, the floor remains clean, dry, and safe, and the quantity is controlled. Best of all, the customer gets a visibly generous portion with great speed, the employee remains efficient and cheerful, and the general impression is one of extravagantly good service.

Mechanized marketing

Consider the other aspects of McDonald's technological approach to marketing. The tissue paper used to wrap each hamburger is color-coded to denote the mix of condiments. Heated reservoirs hold pre-prepared hamburgers for rush demand. Frying surfaces have spatter guards to prevent soiling of the cooks' uniforms. Nothing is left to chance or the employees' discretion.

The entire system is engineered and executed according to a tight technological discipline that ensures fast, clean, reliable service in an atmo-

sphere that gives the modestly paid employees a sense of pride and dignity. In spite of the crunch of eager customers, no employee looks or acts harassed, and therefore no harassment is communicated to the customers.

But McDonald's goes even further. Customers may be discouraged from entering if the building looks unappealing from the outside; hence considerable care goes into the design and appearance of the structure itself.

Some things, however, the architect cannot control, especially at an establishment where people generally eat in their parked cars and are likely to drop hamburger wrappings and empty beverage cartons on the ground. McDonald's has anticipated the requirement: its blacktop parking facilities are dotted like a checkerboard with numerous large, highly visible trash cans. It is impossible to ignore their purpose. Even the most indifferent customer would be struck with guilt if he simply dropped his refuse on the ground. But, just in case he drops it anyway, the larger McDonald's outlets have motorized sweepers for quick and easy cleanup.

What is important to understand about this remarkably successful organization is not only that it has created a highly sophisticated piece of technology, but also that it has done this by applying a manufacturing style of thinking to a people-intensive service situation. If machinery is to be viewed as a piece of equipment with the capability of producing a predictably standardized, customer-satisfying output while minimizing the operating discretion of its attendant, that is what a McDonald's retail outlet is. It is a machine that produces, with the help of totally unskilled machine tenders, a highly polished product. Through painstaking attention to total design and facilities planning, everything is built integrally into the machine itself, into the technology of the system. The only choice available to the attendant is to operate it exactly as the designers intended.

Tooling up for service

Although most people are not aware of it, there are many illustrations of manufacturing solutions to people-intensive service problems. For example:

☐ Mutual funds substitute one sales call for many; one consultation for dozens; one piece of paper for thousands; and one reasonably informed customer choice for numerous, confused, and often poor choices.

☐ Credit cards that are used for making bank loans substitute a single credit decision (issuing the card in the first place) for the many elaborate, costly, people-intensive activities and decisions that bank borrowing generally entails.

☐ Supermarkets substitute fast and efficient self-service for the slow, inefficient, and often erratic clerks of the traditional service store.

In each of these examples a technological device or a manufacturing type of process has replaced what had been resolutely thought of as an irrevocably people-requiring service. Similar devices or processes can be used to modify and alleviate the customer-repelling abrasions of other people-intensive service conditions.

Consider the airlines. This industry is highly unusual. It is exceedingly capital-intensive in the creation of the facilitating product (the airplane), but it is extremely people-intensive in the delivery of the product (travel arrangements and the customer's flight experience). The possibilities for revenue production that a $20-million airplane represents are quickly vitiated by a surly or uncooperative reservations clerk. The potentials of repeat business that the chef so carefully builds into his meals can be destroyed by a dour or sloppy stewardess.

In fact, stewardesses have a particularly dif-

ficult job. A hundred passengers, having paid for reasonable service, understandably expect to be treated with some care. While three young ladies are there to serve them, a number of these passengers must inevitably get their drinks and meals later than others. Most experienced travelers are understanding and tolerant of the rushed stewardesses' problems, but a few usually harass them. The pressure and abuse can easily show in the stewardesses' personal appearance and behavior, and are likely to result in nearly all passengers being reciprocally mistreated. This is human. Besides, the ladies may have been on their feet all day, or may have slept only a few hours the night before.

"More and better training" is not likely to help things very much. When the pressure is on, service deteriorates. And so does a stewardess's cheerful manner and appearance, no matter how well schooled she is in personal care and keeping her cool or how attractively her clothes are designed.

But it might help to put mirrors in the airplane galley, so that each time a stewardess goes in she sees herself. There is some reason to expect that she'll look into the mirror each time she passes it, and that she'll straighten her hair, eliminate that lipstick smudge, put on a more cheerful face. Improvement will be instantaneous. No training needed.

Here is another possibility: the stewardess makes a quick trip down the aisle, passing out rum-flavored bonbons and explaining, "For those who can't wait till we get the ice out." This breaks the tension, produces an air of cheerfulness, acknowledges the passengers' eagerness for quick service, and says that the ladies are trying their hurried best. Further, it brings the stewardess into friendly personal contact with the passenger and reduces the likelihood of her being pressured and abused. She, in turn, is less likely to irritate other passengers.

From the manufacturing point of view, these two modest proposals represent the substitution of tools (or, as I prefer, technology) for motivation. Mirrors are a tool for getting self-motivated, automatic results in the stewardesses' appearance and personal behavior. Bonbons are a tool for creating a benign interpersonal ambience that reduces both the likelihood of customer irritation and the reciprocal and contagious stewardess irritation of others. They are small measures, but so is a company president's plant tour.

In each case there is considerable presumption

of solid benefits. Yet to get these benefits one must think, as the factory engineer thinks, about what the problems are and what the desired output is; about how to redesign the process and how to install new tools that do the job more automatically; and, whenever people are involved, about how to "control" their personal behavior and channel their choices.

Hard & soft technologies

There are numerous examples of strictly "hard" technologies (i.e., pieces of equipment) which are used as substitutes for people—coffee vending machines for waitresses, automatic check-cashing machines for bank tellers, self-operated travel-insurance-policy machines for clerks. Although these devices represent a manufacturing approach to service, and while their principles can be extended to other fields, even greater promise lies in the application of "soft" technologies (i.e., technological systems). McDonald's is an example of a soft technology. So are mutual funds. Other examples are all around us, if we just think of them in the right way. Take the life insurance industry:

A life insurance salesman is said to be in a service industry. Yet what does he really do? He researches the prospect's needs by talking with him, designs several policy models for him, and "consumer-use tests" these models by seek-

ing his reactions. Then he redesigns the final model and delivers it for sale to the customer. This is the ultimate example of manufacturing in the field. The factory is in the customer's living room, and the producer is the insurance

agent, whom we incorrectly think of as being largely a salesman. Once we think of him as a manufacturer, however, we begin to think of how best to design and manufacture the product rather than how best to sell it.

The agent, for example, could be provided with a booklet of overlay sheets showing the insurance plans of people who are similar to the customer. This gives the customer a more credible and informed basis for making a choice. In time, the agent could be further supported by similar information stored in telephone-access computers.

In short, we begin to think of building a system that will allow the agent to produce his product efficiently and effectively by serving the customer's needs instead of performing a manipulative selling job.

Manufacturers outside the factory

The type of thinking just described applies not only to service industries but also to manufacturing industries. When the computer hardware manufacturer provides installation and maintenance services, debugging dry-runs, software programs, and operator training as part of his hardware sales program, he acknowledges that his "product" consists of considerably more than what he made in the factory. What is done in the field is just as important to the customer as the manufactured equipment itself. Indeed, without these services there would generally be no sale.

The problem in so many cases is that customer service is not viewed by manufacturers as an integral part of what the customer buys, but as something peripheral to landing the sale. However, when it is explicitly accepted as integral to the product itself and, as a consequence, gets the same kind of dedicated attention as the manufacture of the hardware gets, the results can be spectacular. For example:

☐ In the greeting card industry, some manufacturer-provided retail display cases have built-in inventory replenishment and reordering features. In effect, these features replace a company salesman with the willing efforts of department managers or store owners. The motivation of the latter to reorder is created by the visible imminence of stockouts, which is achieved with a special color-coded card that shows up as the stock gets low. Order numbers and envelopes are included for reordering. In earlier days a salesman had to call, take inventory, arrange the stock, and write orders. Stock-outs were common.

The old process was called customer service and selling. The new process has no name, and probably has never been viewed as constituting a technological substitute for people. But it is. An efficient, automatic, capital-intensive system, supplemented occasionally by people, has replaced an inefficient and unreliable people-intensive system.

□ In a more complex situation, the A.O. Smith Company has introduced the same kind of preplanning, routinizing, people-conserving activity. This company makes, among other things, grain storage silos that must be locally sold, installed, serviced, and financed. There are numerous types of silos with a great variety of accessories for loading, withdrawing, and automatically mixing livestock feed. The selling is carried out by local distributor-erectors and is a lengthy, difficult, sophisticated operation.

Instead of depending solely on the effective training of distributors, who are spread widely in isolated places, A.O. Smith has developed a series of sophisticated, colorful, and interchangeable design-module planning books. These can be easily employed by a distributor to help a farmer decide what he may need, its cost, and its financing requirements. Easy-to-read tables, broken down by the size of farm, numbers and types of animals, and purpose of animals (cattle for meat or cows for milk), show recommended combinations of silo sizes and equipment for maximum effectiveness.

The system is so thorough, so easy to use and understand, and so effective in its selling capability that distributors use it with great eagerness. As a consequence, A.O. Smith, while sitting in Milwaukee, in effect controls every sales presentation made by every one of its far-flung distributors. Instead of constantly sending costly company representatives out to retrain, cajole, wine-and-dine, and possibly antagonize distributors, the supplier sends out a tool that distributors *want* to utilize in their own self-interest.

Product-line pragmatics

Thinking of service as an integral part of what is sold can also result in alteration of the product itself—and with dramatic results. In 1961, the Building Controls and Components Group of Honeywell, Inc., the nation's largest producer of heating and air conditioning thermostats and control devices, did a major part of its business in replacement controls (the aftermarket). These were sold through heating and air conditioning distributors, who then supplied plumbers and other installation and repair specialists.

At that time, Honeywell's product line consisted of nearly 18,000 separate catalog parts and pieces. The company had nearly 5,000 distributor accounts, none of which could carry a full line of these items economically, and therefore it maintained nearly 100 fully stocked field warehouses that offered immediate delivery to distributors. The result was that, in a large proportion of cases, distributors sold parts to plumbers that they did not themselves have in stock. They either sent plumbers to nearby Honeywell warehouses for pickup or picked up parts themselves and delivered them directly to the plumbers. The costs to Honeywell of carrying these inventories were enormous, but were considered a normal expense of doing business.

Then Honeywell made a daring move—it announced its new Tradeline Policy. It would close all warehouses. All parts would have to be stocked by the distributors. The original equipment, however, had been redesigned into 300 standard, interchangeable parts. These were interchangeable not only for most Honeywell controls, but also for those of its major competitors. Moreover, each package was clearly imprinted to show exactly what Honeywell and competing products were repairable with the contents.

By closing its own warehouses, Honeywell obviously shifted the inventory-carrying costs to its distributors. But instead of imposing new burdens on them, the new product lines, with their interchangeability features, enabled the distributors to carry substantially lower inventories, particularly by cutting down the need for competitive product lines which the distributors could nonetheless continue to service. Thus they were able to offer faster service at lower costs to their customers than before.

But not all distributors were easily persuaded of this possibility, and some dropped the line. Those who were persuaded ultimately proved their wisdom by the enormous expansion of their sales. Honeywell's replacement market share almost doubled, and its original equipment share rose by nearly 50%. Whereas previously nearly 90% of Honeywell's replacement sales were scattered among 4,000 distributors, within ten years after Tradeline's introduction the same proportion (of a doubled volume) was concentrated among only about 900 distributors. Honeywell's cost of servicing these fewer customers was substantially less, its trade inventory carrying costs were cut to zero, and the quality of its distributor services was so substantially improved that only 900 of its distributors captured a larger national market share than did the nearly 4,000 less efficient and more costly distributors.

Again, we see a people-intensive marketing problem being solved by the careful and scru-

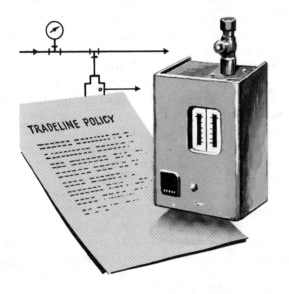

pulous application of manufacturing attitudes. Motivation, hard work, personalization, training, and merchandising incentives were replaced with systematic programming, comprehensive planning, attention to detail, and particularly with imaginative concern for the problems and needs of customers (in this case, the company's distributors).

Stopgaps: complexity...

Exaggeration is not without its merits, especially in love and war. But in business one guards against it with zeal, especially when one tries to persuade oneself. The judicious application of the manufacturing mentality may help the service industries and the customer-service activities of others. Yet this does not necessarily mean the more technology, the better.

Entrepreneurial roadsides are littered with the wrecks of efforts to install Cadillac technologies for people who cannot yet handle the Model T. This point is illustrated by the failure of two exceedingly well-financed joint ventures of highly successful technology companies. These joint ventures attempted to provide computerized

medical diagnostic services for doctors and hospitals. The companies developed console hookups to central diagnostic computers, so that everybody could stop sending off samples to pathology laboratories and agonizingly poring through medical texts to diagnose the patients' symptoms.

The ventures failed because of hospital and doctor resistance, not for want of superior or reliable products. The customer was compelled suddenly to make an enormous change in his accustomed way of doing things, and to employ a strange and somewhat formidable piece of equipment that required special training in its use and in the interpretation of its output.

Interactive teaching machines are meeting a similar fate. The learning results they achieve are uniformly spectacular. The need for improved learning is a visible reality. The demand for greater individualization of teaching is widespread. But the equipment has not sold because technologists have created systems employing equipment that is at the cutting edge of technological progress. The teachers and school systems that must use them are far behind, and already feel badly bruised by their failure to comprehend even simple new technologies. For them, the new Cadillac technologies do not solve problems. They create problems.

... & compromise

On the other hand, failure to exploit technological possibilities can be equally destructive. When a major petroleum company with nearly 30,000 retail outlets in the United States was persuaded to pioneer a revolutionary automobile repair and servicing system, compromises of the original plan ensured the system's failure.

The theory was to build a gigantic service and repair system that could handle heavy volumes of continuous activity by using specialized diagnostic and repair equipment. With this equipment (rather than a harried and overworked man at a gas station) pinpointing the exact problems, cars could be shuttled off to specific stations in the repair center. Experts would work only on one kind of problem and section of a car, with newly designed, fast-action tools. Oil changes would me made in assembly-line fashion by low-paid workers, electrical work would be performed by high-paid technicians doing only that, and a post-diagnostic checkup would be made to guarantee success.

Since profitability would require high volume,

the center would have to draw on a vast population area. To facilitate this, the original proposal called for a specially constructed building at a center-city, old warehouse location—the land would be cheaper, the building would be equally accessible throughout the entire metropolitan area, the service center's technological elegance and see-through windows for customers would offset any run-down neighborhood disadvantages, and volume business would come from planned customer decisions rather than random off-street traffic.

The original concept also called for overnight pickup and delivery service; thus a car could be repaired at night while its owner slept, rather than during the day when he would need it. And because the required promotion of this service would tend to alienate the company's franchised service station dealers, perhaps driving them into the hands of competitors, it was recommended that the first center be installed in a major city where the company had no stations.

This sounds like an excellent manufacturing approach to a service situation; but the company made three fatal compromises:

1. It decided to place the center in a costly, high-traffic suburban location, on the grounds that "if the experiment fails, at least the building will be in a location that has an alternative use." The results were an awkward location, a land-acquisition cost five times higher than the original center-city location, and, therefore, a vastly inflated break-even point for the service center.

2. It decided not to offer overnight service, on the grounds that "we'd better crawl before we walk. And besides, we don't think people will leave their cars overnight in a strange and distant garage." The fact that the results would be guaranteed by a reputable, nationally known petroleum company operating an obviously sophisticated new type of consumer service facility was not persuasive to the corporate decision makers.

3. It decided to put the first center in a city occupied by its own franchised dealers, on the grounds that "we know it better." To offset the problem of not being able to advertise aggressively for business, the company offered its dealers a commission to send their repair jobs to the center. The dealers did this, but only with jobs they could not, or did not want to, do themselves. As a result, the traffic at the big, expensive center was miserably low.

Companies that take a manufacturing approach to service problems are likely to fail if (a) they compromise technological possibilities at the conception and design stage, or (b) they allow technological complexity to contaminate the operating stage. The substitution of technology and systems for people and serendipity is complex in its conception and design; only in its *operation*, as at McDonald's, is it simple.

It is the simplicity of mutual funds that, after all, accounts for their success. But the concept is in fact much more complex than that of selling individual stocks through a single customer-man sitting at a desk. Mutual funds are the financial community's equivalent of McDonald's. They are a piece of technology that not only simplifies life for both the seller and the buyer but also creates many more buyers and makes production more profitable.

Mass merchandising is similar. It substitutes a wide selection and fast, efficient self-service for a narrow selection and slow, incompetent salesclerk service. The mass merchandising retail store (e.g., general merchandise supermarket) is a new technology, incorporating into retailing precisely the thinking that goes into the assembly line, except that the customer does his own assembling.

Why things go wrong

The significance of all this is that a "product" is quite different from what it is generally assumed to be. When asked once what he did, Charles Revson, head of Revlon, Inc., made the now well-known reply, "In the factory we make cosmetics, in the store we sell hope." He defined the product in terms of what the consumer wanted, not in terms of what the manufacturer made. McDonald's obviously does the same—not just hamburgers but also speed, cleanliness, reassurance, cheerfulness, and predictable consistency. Honeywell defined it not in terms of replacement parts but, rather, in terms of those needs of its distributors which, if met, would result in substantially larger proportions of patronage for Honeywell. Thus a product is not something people buy, but a tool they use—a tool to solve their problems or to achieve their intentions.

So many things go wrong because companies fail to adequately define what they sell. Companies in so-called service industries generally think of themselves as offering services rather than manufacturing products; hence they fail to think and act as comprehensively as do manufacturing companies concerned with the efficient, low-cost production of customer-satisfying products.

Moreover, manufacturing companies themselves do not generally think of customer service as an integral part of *their* products. It is an afterthought to be handled by the marketing department.

The marketing department, in turn, thinks of itself as providing customer services. There is a hidden and unintentional implication of giving something away for free. One is doing something extra as a favor. When this is the underlying communication to one's own organization, the result is about what one would expect— casual, discretionary attitudes and little attention to detail, and certainly no attention to the possibilities of substituting systems and preplanning for people and pure effort. Hence products are designed that cannot be easily installed, repaired, or modified.

(Motorola's "works in a box" television set, which has been promoted so successfully on the basis of its easy replacement and repairability, is an outstanding example of the sales-getting potential of proper care in design and manufacturing.)

Chill winds from ice cream

An excellent example of the confusion between what a company "makes" and what a customer "buys" is provided by a producer of private-label ice cream products for supermarket chains. Since supermarkets need to create low-price impressions in order to attract and hold customers, selling successfully to them means getting down to rock-bottom prices. The company (call it the Edwards Company) became extraordinarily good at producing a wide line of ice cream products at rock-bottom costs. It grew rapidly while others went bankrupt. It covered ten states with direct deliveries to stores out of its factory and factory warehouse, but continued growth eventually required establishing plant, distribution, and marketing centers elsewhere. The result was disaster, even though the company manufactured just as efficiently in the new locations as it did in the old.

Under the direct and constant supervision of the president in the original Edwards location, an exceedingly efficient telephone ordering and delivery system had been working to meet the supermarkets' rather stringent requirements. Because of limited storage and display space, they required several-times-a-week delivery at specified, uncrowded store hours. To make up for low volume in slow periods, they needed regular specials as well as holiday and summer specials. Over time, these needs had become so automatically but efficiently supplied from the original Edwards factory location that this delivery service became routinized and therefore taken for granted.

In building the new plant, the president and his compact management team focused on getting manufacturing costs down to rock bottom. After all, that is what made the sale—low prices. Not being very conscious of the fact that they had created in the original location an enormously customer-satisfying, efficient, automatic ordering and delivery system, they did not know exactly what to look for in evaluating how well they were working out these "service" details at the new plant, distribution, and marketing centers.

In short, they did not know what their product really was (why Edwards had become so successful) and they failed to expand Edwards' success. Service was not considered an integral part of the company's product. It was viewed merely as "something else" you do in the business. Accordingly, service received inadequate attention, and that became the cause of the Edwards Company's failure.

Conclusion

Rarely is customer service discretionary. It is a requisite of getting and holding business, just like the generic product itself. Moreover, if customer service is consciously treated as "manufacturing in the field," it will get the same kind of detailed attention that manufacturing gets. It will be carefully planned, controlled, automated where possible, audited for quality control, and regularly reviewed for performance improvement and customer reaction. More important, the same kinds of technological, laborsaving, and systems approaches that now thrive in manufacturing operations will begin to get a chance to thrive in customer service and service industries.

Once service-industry executives and the creators of customer-service programs begin seriously to think of themselves as actually manufacturing a product, they will begin to think like product manufacturers. They will ask: What technologies and systems are employable here? How can things be designed so we can use machines instead of people, systems instead of serendipity? Instead of thinking about better and more training of their customer-service representatives, insurance agents, branch bank managers, or salesmen "out there," they will think about how to eliminate or supplement them.

If we continue to approach service as something done by individuals rather than by machines or systems, we will continue to suffer from two distortions in thinking:

1. Service will be viewed as something residual to the ultimate reality—to a tangible product, to a specific competence (like evaluating loans, writing insurance policies, giving medical aid, preparing on-premises foods). Hence it will have residual respectability, receive residual attention, and be left, somehow, for residual performers.

2. Service will be treated as purely a human task that must inevitably be diagnosed and performed by a single individual working alone with no help or, at best, with the rudimentary help of training and a variety of human-engineering motivators. It will never get the kind of manufacturing-type thinking that goes into tangible products.

Until we think of service in more positive and encompassing terms, until it is enthusiastically viewed as manufacturing in the field, receptive to the same kinds of technological approaches that are used in the factory, the results are likely to be just as costly and idiosyncratic as the results of the lonely journeyman carving things laboriously by hand at home.

Reprint 72505

The industrialization of service

Theodore Levitt

Successful applications
of a new concept can transform
how we behave,
what we do, and where we go

Four years ago in HBR, this author advanced the concept that if companies would stop thinking of service as servitude and personal ministration, they would be able to effect drastic improvements in its quality and efficiency. Now, in this second "service industry" article, he attacks the problem that arose from the first one. Namely, how the ideas of service in the field might be applied to generate "liberating new solutions to intractable old problems."

Mr. Levitt is professor of business administration at the Harvard Business School, where he teaches marketing in the Program for Management Development. A familiar author to HBR readers, this article represents his twentieth appearance in these pages.

Drawings by Robert Pryor.

The service sector of industrially advanced nations has been in ascent for nearly three quarters of a century. In the United States, during the past 15 years alone, the nongoods-producing sector of the nonagricultural labor force rose 52%, versus 38% in the goods-producing sector.

It would be redundant to recite once more the growing share of our GNP that the so-called service sector occupies. Nor is it just the expanding proportions taken up by the multiplicity of government, school-district, and other public employments that have produced this increase, though civilian public employment alone rose 148% in the past 15 years.

Actually, there is a massive hidden service sector—that proportion of nominally "manufacturing" industries so much of whose expenses and revenues represent pre- and postpurchase servicing in the form of systems planning, preinstallation support, "software," repair, maintenance, delivery, collection, bookkeeping, and the like.

As the underdeveloped countries of the world progress and gradually catch up with the more established nations, conventional wisdom has it that the advanced nations will lose their comparative advantage. The shift in the developing nations from craft to industrial labor, and from hand to machine work, produces great increases in productivity.

Meanwhile, in the advanced nations, affluence and discretionary spending shift consumer and industrial demand increasingly into low-productivity, labor-intensive service activities—automotive repair, travel, commercial lodging, entertainment, restaurants, shopping, insurance brokerage, medical care, education, to name a few. The result, so the argument goes, is that the advanced nations lose their advantage even faster than the developing nations expand their manufacturing industries.

In the advanced nations, this has of late produced the paradoxical proposition that their expanding service appetites shift demand in directions that are little susceptible to the employment of mass-production efficiencies. This, in time, leads to rising general price levels and finally to reduced living standards. Since it costs more to buy less-efficiently produced services, one's money doesn't go as far.

Those are the supposed cybernetics of world economics—advantage leads ultimately to a demand for costly service amenities while producing a parallel no-frills catch-up effort among the less advantaged. The latter, finally, not only catch up but surpass the original leaders because, for one reason, their technology is more modern.

Japan, Germany, and Hong Kong are dramatic examples of no-frills catch-up. Britain is a dismal example of a country that has been caught up on and now has been left pathetically behind.

Britain is also a particularly apt example for showing that the fears of accelerating disadvantage and reduced living standards in the more advanced, service-intensive industrial nations are not necessarily justified. Britain shows, particularly by comparison with the United States, that the rising proportion of GNP devoted to so-called "service" activities does not necessarily produce a parallel and equivalent decline in either absolute or relative productivity.

In the United States, the service sector has demonstrated a remarkable capacity to improve productivity, while in Britain it has exhibited the polar opposite—an almost obsessive persistence of ancient service practices that drain the economy of competitive vitality. In Britain, the word "serve" remains to this day encrusted with immemorial attachments to master-servant pretensions that dull the imagination and block the path to service efficiency.

For example, in spite of spectacularly rising British retail prices, laws have recently been passed to resist the construction and growth of that marvel of retailing efficiency, the huge self-service hypermarché.

More efficient even than the American supermarket and the general-merchandise mass marketer, the hypermarché has been effectively resisted by coalitions of small personal-service retailers and local and national politicians.

This kind of resistance to retailing efficiency reflects a profoundly persistent cultural manifestation with its ancestral roots in distant centuries. Historically, the way to "serve" was in the form of one person for the benefit of another—the butler, the footman, the parlor maid, the upstairs maid, the solicitor, the butcher, the greengrocer, the tailor, and the cook—each performing one-on-one, highly personalized service, whether laying out the clothes or cutting the roast just right to the exacting specifications of each familiar customer.

To this day, even moderately priced restaurants in various parts of the world are redundantly populated with paid factotums in frayed sartorial imitations of the past, each specializing in a separate and costly triviality like opening doors, removing and carrying coats to the cloakroom (manned by yet another), or removing dirty ashtrays (but not also dirty dishes) from tables. And in business offices, the prodigality of worn-out and outworn retainers ever present to run errands and perform menial personal services is visible everywhere, doing questionably required work that incurs unquestionably real expense and serves no real purpose.

Things add up, not only in their measurable pecuniary costs, but also in the way people think about the work to be done, and how to do it.

As I have said in my previous "service industry" article, as long as we cling to preindustrial notions about what service is and does, none of the applied rationality which has produced such magnificent efficiencies in the industrial system will be brought to bear on what remains today a maze of inefficiencies in the service sectors that surround that system.[1]

The foregoing examples of service wastefulness still present in many countries illustrate a general rule about endurance: things may be obsolescent though not obsolete. Service may be less wasteful in the United States; but to the extent that ancient fetters do enthrall our attitudes toward, and shape the quality of, service work, everywhere their endurance carries a single common presumption. Namely, that service literally means, and will be best, when one

person directly and personally attends another, much like that of servant and master. And so long as this presumption reigns, service will forever be limited in efficiency, reliability, and quality.

Opportunities for service improvement lie all around and yet in the United States, where much improvement has already occurred, these have gone vastly unnoticed. We celebrate the glamorous work of heroic astronauts, accomplishing through science and technology deeds of speculative merit. But we ignore the practical accomplishments of people who produce with lesser tools, simpler methods, and less elaborate organization, a constant stream of productive service results of more mundane though immediate merit.

In this article, I hope to show exactly how amply we are benefited by so much we daily see but don't apprehend, how these benefactions are the result of what I call the "industrialization of service," but also how, by way of concrete examples, our service activities still lag far behind existing potentials for improving their efficiency and productivity.

Service fecundity

Go back to the hypermarché. Its forerunners in the United States are supermarkets and mass-merchandising discount stores. These are self-service stores, and that explains their superior retailing effectiveness. Instead of yesterday's corner grocery store clerk behind the counter responding to each customer's special requests for items that had to be individually fetched, weighed, and bagged, today's supermarket customer does most of the work alone, moving through the aisles assembling the purchase from the store inventory much as an automobile frame moves along a production line and gets assembled from the plant inventory.

The supermarket represents the industrialization of an ancient retail service, much as the assembly line represents the industrialization of ancient craftsmanship. In both cases, there are tremendous economies, great efficiencies, and much better products. For example, I would insist that the modern automobile *is* better—more uniformly reliable, comparatively cheaper, more durable, and yet still highly customized to the specifications of millions of in-

1. See "Production-line Approach to Service," HBR September-October 1972, p 41.

dividual buyers, each with his private preferences that get rather satisfactorily served at low costs.

The independent craftsman might have constructed a more personalized and interesting car, but also probably a more idiosyncratic one, embellishing the whole project with elaborate little pirouettes expressing his own style—perhaps quaintly ornamented or disastrously experimental. And so with the butcher at the older store. He might have cut the roast more lovingly (or more shrewdly), and perhaps have augmented it with the self-serving weight of his thumb on the scale. Certainly, his was a more personal production, but also less predictably reliable and probably more painfully costly.

Industrializing modes

The supermarket represents one industrialization of service. It combines more space and capital in larger but fewer aggregates. Gone, for the most part, are the ancient modes of "service" it displaced with new efficiencies, lower costs, and greater customer satisfaction. Altogether, it is an efficient act of creative destruction.

There are numerous other ways in which service has already been industrialized. While most people regularly see them at work, few are aware of them. Even fewer fully appreciate their revolutionizing importance for our lives and businesses. Thus it is worth a close look at the industrializing modes which already help make service more abundantly productive than it has been in the past. It will help focus effort and energize activity toward the use of these principles in other service activities.

Service can be industrialized in three ways: via hard, soft, and hybrid technologies.

Hard technologies

These are the most obvious—they substitute machinery, tools, or other tangible artifacts for people-intensive performance of service work. Thus:

1

The electrocardiogram reliably substitutes a lower-paid technician for the higher-paid doctor listening with a stethoscope.

2

The consumer credit card and CRT credit and bank-balance checking machine replace a time-consuming manual credit check for each purchase.

3

Airport X-ray surveillance equipment replaces a lengthy and often embarrassing manual rummage through baggage.

4

The automatic car wash and hot wax coating replace the uneven quality and dignity-destroying work of individuals washing and waxing by hand.

5

The Polaroid Land camera replaces film that must be returned and processed in an essentially people-intensive plant.

6

Automatic coin receptacles at bridges, subway entrances, toll roads, and elsewhere replace human collectors.

7

And the home is full of hard technologies—automatic washers, precooked convenience foods, never-needs-ironing clothing, and chemically treated dirt-resistant clothing, floor covering, and upholstered furniture.

Soft technologies

These are essentially the substitution of organized preplanned systems for individual service operatives. Often these involve some modification of the tools (or technologies) employed, but their essential feature is the system itself, where special hardware or routines are specifically designed to produce the desired results. Consider:

1

Supermarkets and other establishments like cafeterias, restaurant salad bars, open tool rooms in factories, and open-stack libraries that enable people to serve themselves quickly and efficiently.

2

Fast-food restaurants, like McDonald's, Burger Chef, Pizza Hut, Dunkin' Donuts, or Kentucky Fried Chicken. At each the same rational system of division of labor and specialization is rigorously followed to produce speed, quality control, cleanliness, and low prices.

3

Prepackaged vacation tours that obviate the need for time-consuming personal selling, extensive tailoring of the product to numerous different kinds of customers, and a great deal of price haggling.

American Express probably has the largest variety of packages that are handsomely presented, de-

scribed, and promoted in a brochure of magazine proportions. Significantly this, too, is like an assembly line in principle. American Express neither creates nor operates the tours; that's done by others. American Express merely assembles and packages the information and sells the product for those who deliver it.

4

Off-the-shelf insurance programs—packaged and unalterable, except via the selection of other packages. Allstate Insurance was the mass-market pioneer, though preceded by the old "industrial" insurance salesman who sold door-to-door and collected weekly, and more recently imitated by off-the-shelf insurance-by-mail.

5

Mutual funds instead of one-at-a-time stock selection, the latter filled with ambiguities, uncertainties, and repetitive reselling and reeducation with each transaction.

6

Christmas Club and payroll-deduction savings systems, both one-time selling and one-time deciding situations, and thereafter automatically, routinely, and inexpensively executed.

7

Fully systematized, production-line, yet personalized income tax preparation service on a walk-in basis—performed at low cost with remarkable accuracy and guarantees. The pioneer and master merchant is, of course, H. & R. Block.

Hybrid technologies
These combine hard equipment with carefully planned industrial systems to bring efficiency, order, and speed to the service process. To illustrate:

1

Computer-based over-the-road truck routing. By careful programming for types and grades of roads, location of stops, congestion of roads, toll-road costs, and mixing-point access, the system optimizes truck utilization and minimizes user cost. Its most extensive and complex incarnation is Cummins Engine's "Power Management Program."

2

Radio controlled ready-mix concrete truck routing, rerouting, and delivery—pioneered early and to an advanced state by Texas Industries of Dallas.

3

Development of unit trains and integral trains that carry, over long distances, only a single commodity (e.g., coal by the Baltimore and Ohio Railroad; grain by the Illinois Central) with few or no intermediate stops. By providing fast long runs at enormous efficiency, the trains can dead-head back and still save money.

In the case of the B&O, its original unit train reduced the round-trip time between West Virginia's coal fields and Baltimore from 21 to 7 days.

4

Preorder shipment of perishables at long distance. The system was pioneered by Sunkist to send train-loads of lemons from California east before orders have been placed, using weather forecasting services for intermediate routing and drop-offs in time to reach cities where expected high temperatures will raise the consumption of lemonade and Tom Collinses. Any lost hot day is a lost day of sales.

Weyerhaeuser developed a similar system for shipping lumber east to provide an inventory-free "instant" delivery capability to distant customers.

5

Limited-service, fast, low-priced repair facilities, such as national muffler and transmission shops. Pioneered by Midas, this system features high volume, specialization, and special-purpose tools which combine to produce fast, guaranteed results.

All of the foregoing are fairly familiar, though seldom recognized, examples of hard, soft, and hybrid technologies (that is, of machines and organized work systems or combinations thereof) at work in what was always done before as an extension of the craft culture, or in a primitive industrial fashion that merely substituted a more powerful or efficient machine (say, the locomotive or the steam shovel) for a weaker or less capacious predecessor (say, the horse or the spade).

Special opportunities

Fortunately, there is a huge array of additional service possibilities, some of them not nearly so ob-vious as to their potential, and many considerably more promising than even their visible potential at first suggests. The failure of so many people to recognize that such opportunities exist, or even to appreciate successful applications already made, is a measure of how inexorably we remain tethered to the fetters of an ancient heritage, and therefore unalert to the possibilities of the application of those same disciplines to what yet remains to be done.

Principle of magnitude

"You just can't get reliable repair service any more" is such a persistent national refrain that one is immediately justified in automatically doubting whether it's true. When the General Electric Service Corporation's clean white radio-dispatched repair truck pulls into my driveway, I *know* I am going to get better and more reliable TV service than in the old days of the under-inventoried variably priced TV shop, and its questionably trained serviceman in a battered pickup truck.

Similarly, I am very much reassured at the Exxon repair center where there are twelve fully equipped, fully lighted, temperature-controlled work stations and uniformed certified mechanics, and where prices are posted, estimates made clearly in advance, and the completed work is ready when promised.

Yet it is precisely these kinds of service activities that have room for the most improvement. But they require as a precondition to high efficiency and low cost the same sorts of disciplines and strategies that make modern manufacturing so efficient and low-cost—the employment of (a) industrial modes of thinking to the organization of the service effort, and often (b) large amounts of capital.

For the Exxon repair center to be efficient it requires, first, division of labor. A trained transmission expert worth $8 an hour must not work at such low-wage jobs as changing transmission oil. Nor would one let a low-wage oil-changer try to repair the transmission.

In order to enjoy the advantages of division of labor, one needs considerable volume. That requires a large plant, which occupies lots of land and is fully equipped with costly new labor-saving tools and diagnostic and repair machinery. Also, the plant has to be professionally managed, and promoted and advertised with sufficient frequency and persuasibility to draw large numbers of motorists from a wide area. This would, in turn, probably require pickup and delivery services to make up for the inconvenience of motorists having to come long distances. All this is costly.

Thus efficiency in service can require as much costly investment in plant, land, equipment, and promotion as has been historically associated with efficiency in manufacturing. It can require as much planning, organization, training, control, and management as that used to produce the original car. It requires, in short, a different way of thinking about what service is, what it can become, and how it must be financed.

The key point is "volume"—in a magnitude sufficient to achieve efficiency and to employ systems and technologies which produce reliable, rapid, and low unit-cost service results. And that, in turn, requires the kind of managerial rationality seldom seen (or, indeed, needed) in a small shop.

This same principle of magnitude applies in other highly promising areas where its employment is now in its infancy. For example:

1
Specialized, highly automated medical diagnostic clinics. The Damon Corporation in Needham Heights, Massachusetts, operates 125 such clinics throughout the nation which, with the help of modern machines, 125 salaried M.D.s, 22 Ph.D.s, and 1,400 medical technologists, perform a wide range of diagnostic tests that formerly required patients to visit several doctors and clinics at costs in time and money several multiples above those of Damon's.

2
Prepaid health service centers, consisting of a wide range of specialists who can be kept fully employed at their specialties. Pioneered by the Kaiser Foundation in Oakland, California, there are several hundred Health Maintenance Organizations all over the country. Members prepay annual "dues" for easy access to full-time medical specialists and technicians working in central clinics (equipped with the latest technologies) at their respective specialties, and only their specialties.

Nor is low-cost, rapid, convenient health care confined to out-patient services. Since the formation of the first Ambulatory Surgical Facility in Phoenix, Arizona, in 1970, there are now nearly 100 ASFs in the United States. These are normally equipped to

do some 125 low-risk operations on patients. The typical facility has two or more operating rooms, a recovery area, and a diagnostic center. The patient comes in (say for a tonsillectomy), undergoes tests and surgery, rests, and goes home—all in one day.

For example, at Northwest Surgicare, a for-profit ASF in the Chicago area, the total tonsillectomy bill is $169, compared with $548 at Chicago's not-for-profit Michael Reese Hospital. The Metropolitan Insurance Company, which honors 22 ASFs under group insurance policies, estimates it has saved $1 million in the past three years.

3
Word processing—the new (and not yet entirely successful) system of centralized typing for offices, including the use of computerized self-correcting typewriters. Instead of numerous erratically busy secretaries scattered throughout a large company's offices, a great deal of routine typing is centralized into continually busy word-processing centers where the fastest equipment becomes justified, and scheduling and supervision become sensible.

4
Centralized food preparation commissaries, providing fresh and tasty delicatessen foods and sandwiches to large numbers of small convenience stores, private clubs, or offices. In some cases (e.g., Stewart Infra-Red, Inc., Fontana, Wisconsin), these commissaries have route delivery systems and provide infrared and microwave ovens to their customers.

Product/repair interface

Another special opportunity for service improvement resides in the design of products that often require postpurchase servicing. I call this the product/repair interface. Perhaps the best known solution to this repair-service problem is Motorola's (now Quasar's) highly advertised "works in a drawer" television design. Instead of emphasizing improved repair capability via the ancient idea that to get better service requires getting better, or better training of, servicemen, Motorola simply eliminated the serviceman—or nearly so.

Designed as a modular assembly, the Motorola television set is capable of "instant" reparation by simply removing and replacing a major module that contains a defective part. A direct imitation of the military's concept of "third echelon maintenance," it emphasizes fast restoration.

The military was clear enough about its needs—fast and reliable return to urgent duty at the front. So was Motorola—get the TV set working reliably fast. By originally designing the product with that in mind, the company not only produced great sales appeal, but also discovered that this very orientation and intention enabled it to design a quite efficient, low-cost television set.

Yet, despite the exceptional example, even the most cursory examination of industrial equipment tells a prodigal tale of miniscule attention to the postpurchase repair and maintenance problem. No wonder "service costs so much"; no wonder "service takes so much time"; no wonder "service is so awful."

Recent achievements

Ideas and concepts are often easier understood in principle than translated into actuality. Some translations are easy enough to recognize and, in retrospect, easy enough to comprehend as representing the industrialization of service. Here are a few less obvious examples worth a look:

Paperwork problem

The Transamerica Title Insurance Company receives thousands of applications each week from numerous small field offices on the West Coast, in the Southwest, and from Colorado and Michigan. Clerks and "escrow officers" handle these applications, for which careful title searches through old property records must be made to guarantee the buyer (and protect the lender) against postpurchase claims against the seller.

The preparation of these preliminary policies required endless telephone calls, a constant and irregular stream of documentation, and frequent requests for speedy action, clarification, resolution of complaints, and help from the many parties to any single transaction—buyer, seller, listing real estate broker, selling real estate broker, lender, tax collectors, surveyors, and termite inspectors.

And in all this maelstrom of noise and activity, exact calculations had to be made regarding the allocation of credits and debits for prorated proportions of re-

maining taxes, interest, and other assessments; instructions had to be issued regarding each party's remaining duties and where and how these were to be discharged; and all these procedures had to be done efficiently, rapidly, without error, and for numerous accounts by each escrow officer all day long, all week long.

Now, Transamerica has systematically industrialized much of this complex, pressure-cooker process. By carefully analyzing the various functions performed and classifying them by degree of importance, such as the thoroughness of title search and being absolutely error-proof in the "closing" of the transaction and in the insurance policy, the work was divided into several distinct tasks.

Instead of each office person doing everything, or a major part of everything, separate installations have been created where some specialists do only title searches, some only the auditing, others only the typing of the "closing" papers, and still others only the policy issuance. Productivity and accuracy have improved dramatically. Currently in process is the computerization of required financial calculations and typing.

Meanwhile, in order to guard against the erosion of standards and workmanship that routinization so often produces, systems of work-assignment rotation have been installed. In addition, employment career ladders have been created that give the various specialized workers opportunities for advancement and self-development.

Shoe repair problem

D. Hilston Ryan, product manager of an American packaged-goods company in Europe, got impatient with a two-week wait to have new heels put on a pair of his shoes. So he and an associate designed a fast-service shoe repair facility. With no equipment available to meet the needs as they visualized them, they persuaded a manufacturer to produce equipment to their specifications. It was designed to apply two new heels and soles in less than two minutes.

Then, they persuaded the largest department store in Brussels to put their fast-service, while-you-wait, 40-square-foot shop into the store window on opening day. Lines formed for two blocks. Within four years, they had 1,400 leased installations in department stores, railroad stations, and supermarkets all over Europe.

What was the secret? They invented a speedy repair system—not only in the design of the equipment, but also in the location of inventory relative to the location of the specialized equipment. There were seating arrangements for the while-you-wait customers so they could see the work being done. Of great importance, the system featured low-noise machines and automatic dust collectors to prevent polluting both the shop area and the surrounding store. And the prices charged the customers? Lower, of course.

Selling problem

Few things trouble the business community more than the alleged high and accelerating "cost of selling," especially of personal selling. There are, of course, solutions, and I have mentioned some: self-service stores, which simply eliminate the personal selling function; mutual funds which substitute one sales call for many; packaged travel tours, which substitute planned itineraries for negotiated ones; and, in industrial selling, there is an abundance of item and parts catalogues which facilitate self-service ordering.

There is also the enormous explosion of highly sophisticated direct-mail and catalog selling, direct-response selling via order forms in newspapers and magazines, and direct-response selling via telephone or television solicitation.

The significance of some of these cases is that the products and the product lines are a direct consequence of the media that are available for their sale. Thus certain forms of life, casualty, and hospitalization insurance were created specifically to be sold via mail, newspapers, or television. The same is true of a large number of music record albums, even of companies such as the $87-million-a-year K-Tel Corporation which was specifically organized for television-telephone response merchandising.

Indeed, telephone solicitation and selling have suddenly boomed into one of the great hidden forms of modern selling. In 1975, each day an average of 7 million U.S. consumers answered their telephones to someone who wanted to ask them, offer them, or sell them something. Nearly 3 million of them—homemakers or businesspeople—agreed to listen, and 460,000 completed the offered proposition then and there at an average purchase price of $60, for a total of $28 million per day, or nearly $6 billion worth of sales a year.

The first mass-marketing telephone campaign was undertaken more than a decade ago by Ford Motor Company and directed by Murray Roman, chairman today of Campaign Communications Institute of America, Inc. (CCI), probably the world's foremost specialist in offering telephone marketing services. Twenty million telephone calls were made by 15,000 housewives hired and trained to do the job from their own homes. Following a carefully programmed script, they called a million households a day to determine good prospects for an automobile purchase. On the average, each call took less than one minute.

The campaign generated 340,000 leads (2 per day for each of Ford's 23,000 dealer salesmen), 187,000 of which were "valid" in that the prospects proved to be actively interested in buying within six months. A total of 40,000 units of sales were attributable to the program for a $24 million incremental profit before the telephone campaign cost of $2.8 million.[2]

All Bell Telephone companies have specialists and trainers available gratis to their users for advising and training individuals and small groups on improved techniques and procedures of telephone marketing. Telephone marketing, like most things, is a craft that uses tools and techniques that can be learned. Every aspect of the task—caller recruitment, training, call programming, working conditions, and key phrases for getting results—should be carefully planned and executed as though it happens on an automotive assembly line.

Companies of all kinds in almost all industries increasingly use this medium, usually with the help of specialists in its use for such purposes as selling and taking orders, qualifying leads, motivating delinquent accounts, upgrading marginal customers, reactivating old customers, finding and screening for new business, delivering taped messages to selected audiences, raising funds for institutions or public causes, and of course getting out the vote.

With the availability of Wide Area Telephone Service (WATS lines), FX calls, 800-numbers (inbound WATS), and declining long-distance telephone charges, telephone selling that is organized with production-line rationality has become a major means for the industrialization of various kinds of selling and sales-related communications, particularly as postal rates and personal-selling costs rise.

2. Source of statistics in this paragraph and the details of how telephone selling has been and can be industrialized are in the forthcoming book, by Murray Roman, *Telephone Marketing: How to Build Your Business by Telephone* (New York: McGraw-Hill).

End-use specialization

The computer industry has gone perhaps further than most in specializing its activities to the requirements of specific uses and industries. Among mainframe producers, specialization has centered on selling, programming, and equipment servicing, with salesmen and programmers specializing not by equipment, but rather by customer industries and applications. Though it is not usually viewed as such, this division of labor represents the same kinds of rational specialization so productive in other industries.

The particular value of citing the computer industry is that it views "service" as central to the total product package, in part because (especially in the beginning) prospects and customers were almost totally uninformed about what computers could do and how to use them. Therefore, service became an essential part of the product itself.

Specialization of the sales forces, the programming, and the hardware services produced computer sales and customer-satisfying results in proportions far beyond those achieved by companies that did not specialize. Specialization is to service what division of labor is to manufacturing—the first step to low-cost, reliable abundance.

Cyrus McCormick pioneered the idea, putting demonstration salesmen to work on wheat farms and providing repairmen in the field. DuPont pioneered with applications specialists in the textile and garment industries. In these cases, the "product" that was offered by the "salesmen" consisted less of what was manufactured in the factory than of what was provided by way of practical help and advice in the field. In effect, service *was* the product, and still today in many situations it remains more the product than meets the eye. Customers don't buy things; they buy tools to solve problems. Specialists who know the customer's problems are more likely to provide solutions than those who only know the equipment.

The idea of specialization is actually more common than we are aware. For example, we have become so accustomed to seeing savings and loan institutions standing cheek-by-jowl with commercial banks that we fail to note that each is a separate financial institution organized specifically to specialize in respect to separate markets. Thus savings and loan banks largely provide mortgage financing to residential home buyers, while commercial banks provide a wider range of short-term money-related services.

Dozens of other examples abound: specialty retail stores (shoes, health and beauty aids, books, sporting goods); specialty service stores (dry cleaning, insurance, realty); oil exploration companies (drillers, seismic testing, core analysis); a vast variety of computer companies (soft-ware, data-base, processing); chemical and medical testing companies; investment advisory and fulfillment institutions; and many others.

The list is long and varied. It is trying to tell us something. Namely, that narrow functional specialization has the virtue of focusing energy and attention rather than their getting whirled centrifugally into uncontrolled and uncontrollable bits and pieces where management attention and talent are spread too thinly over too much.

Discovery & explication

Exactly two hundred years ago, Adam Smith gave a name to the kind of specialization and concentration I have been talking about. It has traveled in manufacturing and economics ever since under one name: division of labor. The difference in the examples just cited is that this division has become embodied in separate institutions and products—companies specializing in the "labors" into which they divided themselves, and in the products created around those divided labors.

Thus what we witness is nothing particularly new. What *is* new is the suggestion that the accidents of evolution which created these institutional specialists and product specializations in service can be explained and contemplated in the context of what I call "industrialization." The managerial rationality embodied in the practical imagination we see exercised so effectively everywhere in manufacturing can, given the effort, be applied with similarly munificent results in the service industries.

We are seeing the practical possibilities of the industrialization of service, which has in fact existed in some form for thousands of years, but has recently been pressing forward with accelerating tempo. Once we understand the underlying reason for the success and growth of these service institutions and products, and that they have a common and explicable rationality, we grasp the potential of having in the world of commerce and industry the revolutionizing impact that Antoine Lavoisier had in chemistry and life.

Lavoisier overthrew the ancient phlogistic doctrine in chemistry with his discovery of oxygen and its role in combustion. Everybody had seen that "air" helps things burn, but scientifically the phenomenon had been mystified rather than explicated. Once explicated, though the phenomenon had existed since Prometheus, it became the foundation of modern chemistry.

The ink with which these words are written, the paper on which they are printed, the polyester clothes in which the reader is dressed, the polypropylene rugs on which he or she walks, the medicines he takes—all owe their existence to Lavoisier's discovery of a phenomenon that man had always known and used to sustain life. But his discovery and explication of exactly what made that life possible subsequently transformed and emancipated human life.

So it may very well be with the concept of industrialization. It is an explanation of what the historic and now accelerating specialization in service is, practically speaking, all about. Man lives not by bread alone, but mostly by catch words. What he believes and feels in his mind and emotions are more deterministic than what is in his physical possession.

It is critical to understand and get into our minds that the kinds of successful specializations of effort in the nongoods-producing sectors of our world that I have described represent a uniquely organized set of processes. These are in fact the industrialization of activities long thoughtlessly assumed as inaccessible to the functional rationality (call it "management") that has produced so much low-cost abundance in the goods-producing sectors of the world's more advanced economies. Thus to recognize and understand this phenomenon for what it is in practical terms is to introduce a potentially emancipating new cognitive mode and operating style into modern enterprise.

The concept of industrialization of service, once it enters our minds—though we have unknowingly lived with it since the beginning of mortal time—can transform how we behave, what we do, and where we go. It can generate liberating new solutions to intractable old problems. It can bring to the increasingly service-dominated economies of the future the same kinds of vaulting advances in productivity and living standards as the newly created goods-producing factory economies brought to the world in the past.

Reprint 76506

READ THE FINE PRINT

REPRINTS
Telephone: 617-495-6192
Fax: 617-495-6985

Current and past articles
are available, as is an
annually updated index.
Discounts apply to
large-quantity purchases.

Please send orders to
HBR Reprints
Harvard Business School
Publishing Division
Boston, MA 02163.

HOW CAN *HARVARD BUSINESS REVIEW* ARTICLES WORK FOR YOU?

For years, we've printed a microscopically small notice on the editorial credits page of the *Harvard Business Review* alerting our readers to the availability of *HBR* articles.

Now we invite you to take a closer look at some of the many ways you can put this hard-working business tool to work for you.

IN THE CORPORATE CLASSROOM.

There's no more effective, or cost-effective, way to supplement your corporate training programs than in-depth, incisive *HBR* articles.

Affordable and accessible, it's no wonder hundreds of companies and consulting organizations use *HBR* articles as a centerpiece for management training.

IN-BOX INNOVATION.

Where do your company's movers and shakers get their big ideas? Many find the inspiration for innovation in the pages of *HBR*. They then share the wealth and spread the word by distributing *HBR* articles to company colleagues.

IN MARKETING AND SALES SUPPORT.

HBR articles are a substantive leave-behind to your sales calls. And they can add credibility to your direct mail campaigns. They demonstrate that your company is on the leading edge of business thinking.

CREATE CUSTOM ARTICLES.

If you want to pack even greater power in your punch, personalize *HBR* articles with your company's name or logo. And get the added benefit of putting your organization's name before your customers.

AND THERE ARE 500 MORE REASONS IN THE *HBR CATALOG.*

In all, the *Harvard Business Review Catalog* lists articles on over 500 different subjects. Plus, you'll find books and videos on subjects you need to know.

The catalog is yours for just $8.00. To order *HBR* articles or the *HBR Catalog* (No. 21019), call 617-495-6192. Please mention telephone order code 025A when placing your order. Or FAX us at 617-495-6985.

And start putting *HBR* articles to work for you.

Harvard Business School Publications

Call 617-495-6192 to order the *HBR Catalog.*

(Prices and terms subject to change.)

YOU SAID: AND WE SAID:

❝Give us training tools that are relevant to our business...ones we can use *now*.❞

❝We need new cases that stimulate meaningful discussion.❞

❝It can't be a catalog of canned programs... everything we do is custom.❞

❝Make it a single source for up-to-date materials ...on the most current business topics.❞

❝Better yet if it's from a reputable business school. That adds credibility.❞

❝Introducing the Harvard Business School Publications Corporate Training and Development Catalog.❞

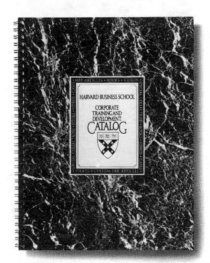

You asked for it. And now it's here.

The Harvard Business School Publications Corporate Training and Development Catalog is created exclusively for those who design and develop custom training programs.

It's filled cover-to-cover with valuable materials you can put to work on the spot. You'll find a comprehensive selection of cases, *Harvard Business Review* articles, videos, books, and more.

Our new catalog covers the critical management topics affecting corporations today, like Leadership, Quality, Global Business, Marketing, and Strategy, to name a few. And it's all organized, indexed, and cross-referenced to make it easy for you to find precisely what you need.

Harvard Business School Publications

HOW TO ORDER.

To order by FAX, dial 617-495-6985. Or call 617-495-6192. Please mention telephone order code 132A. Or send this coupon with your credit card information to: HBS Publications Corporate Training and Development Catalog, Harvard Business School Publishing Division, Operations Department, Boston, MA 02163. **All orders must be prepaid.**

Order No.	Title	Qty. ×	Price +	Shipping* =	Total
39001	Catalog		$8		

Prices and terms subject to change.
*For orders outside Continental U.S.: 20% for surface delivery. Allow 3-6 months. *Express Deliveries* billed at cost; all foreign orders not designating express delivery will be sent by surface mail.

☐ VISA   ☐ American Express   ☐ MasterCard

Card Number_____ Exp. Date_____

Signature_____

Telephone_____ FAX_____

Name_____

Organization_____

Street_____

City_____ State/Zip_____

Country_____ ☐ Home Address ☐ Organization Address

Please Reference Telephone Order Code 132A